T0246242

The Crab Pot Cookbook

The Crab Pot Cookbook

Boat-to-Table Recipes from Seattle's Iconic Waterfront Restaurant

Published by Flashpoint™ Books, Seattle
www.flashpointbooks.com

Produced by Girl Friday Productions

Design: Paul Barrett
Production editorial: Laura Dailey
Project management: Kristin Duran

Image credits: Front cover (clockwise from top left): Shutterstock (SS)/MERCURY studio, Sean Fischer, SS/Brent Hofacker, iStock/THEPALMER. Back cover (top): James Schay. Back cover (bottom): Jerry Petersen. Page 6: iStock/THEPALMER, 10–11: SS/Michael J Magee, 12: SS/Ryan C Slimak, 14: SS/JSim2018, 16–17: MOHAI, PEMCO Webster & Stevens Collection, 1983.10.6182, 19: MOHAI, Courtesy of the Seattle Municipal Archives, 20: Courtesy of the Seattle Municipal Archives, 21 (top): Courtesy of the Seattle Municipal Archives, 21 (bottom): Courtesy of the Seattle Municipal Archives, 22–23: Courtesy of the Seattle Municipal Archives, 24: Sean Fischer, 26–27: Sean Fischer, 28: Sean Fischer, 30–31: Jerry Petersen, 34: SS/Joanna K-V, 37: Sean Fischer, 41: SS/Taras Shparhala, 43: Mike Hipple, 53: SS/AAScott, 56: SS/Ashley-Belle Burns, 59: SS/Irina Burakova, 60: SS/Veranika848, 72: SS/kazoka, 74: SS/YVETTE BARNETT, 77: SS/Cavan-Images, 81: SS/Rui Palma, 93: SS/JeniFoto, 94: SS/DONOT6_STUDIO, 97–101: Jerry Petersen, 107: SS/deden iman, 110: SS/Kevin Cass, 113: SS/Sergey Uryadnikov, 114: SS/Vasik Olga, 122: SS/weera sreesam, 124: SS/Mati Nitibhon, 132: SS/JMP_Traveler, 135: SS/Ludovic Farine, 138: SS/Aleksander Kuzznetsoff, 141: SS/kazucha, 142: SS/Gaus Alex, 145: SS/In Green, 173: SS/Jason Kolenda, 175: SS/Mitchell Coyle Photo, 176: SS/Zhukova Valentyna, 178–179: Jerry Petersen, 191: Thomas D. Petersen, 192: Jerry Petersen. Crab illustrations (cover and throughout interior): iStock/IADA. All other images © James Schay.

ISBN (hardcover): 978-1-959411-50-5
ISBN (ebook): 978-1-959411-51-2

Library of Congress Control Number: 2023916147

First edition

To our hardworking employees of the Crab Pot restaurants in Seattle and Bellevue, Washington, and Long Beach, California

Contents

Introduction

Fishmongers call out to each other at historic Pike Place Market as they

toss freshly caught salmon across the ice. The aroma of espresso wafts from the original Starbucks storefront across the street. These and the myriad other waterfront attractions inundate the senses along Seattle's waterfront: bike taxi drivers ringing bells as they weave around pedestrians, ferries blowing whistles as commuters depart for nearby islands, and blue herons soaring above a cluster of harbor seals lazily floating in the water. To the south, giant port cranes hoist containers onto barges while, to the north, enormous cruise ships set sail for Alaska. And sailboats of all sizes crisscross the sparkling blue waters of Elliott Bay.

But perhaps the best sights and sounds along the water come from the children giggling in delight at so many things for them to see and do: make faces at frisky sea otters at the Seattle Aquarium, board a tour boat to watch for whales, ride an old-fashioned carousel or a giant Ferris wheel, and browse curiosity shops for trinkets to take home. And, of course, the entire family can also enjoy some of the best seafood in the city at the Crab Pot Restaurant on Pier 57.

Seattle's Central Waterfront: Past and Present

Long before tourists began to discover the sumptuous flavors of Pacific Northwest seafood, hundreds of thousands of Indigenous people lived along Puget Sound. This magnificent body of water, which is part of the larger Salish Sea that connects the state of Washington to British Columbia and empties into the Pacific Ocean through the Strait of Juan de Fuca, has been home to the Duwamish, Muckleshoot, Nisqually, Skagit, Snoqualmie, Suquamish, and other tribes for hundreds of years.

The Puget Sound region has also been home to an extensive range of mammals, birds, and marine life. It is here that humpback whales and orcas can be seen breaching, Dall's porpoises can be found congregating, and California sea lions can be spotted gliding along the shorelines in search of food. It is also through these waters that many of the iconic Pacific salmon travel on their way out to the ocean and, eventually, back again to the rivers where they hope to spawn.

The Indigenous tribes who lived in this region, collectively known as the Coast Salish, discovered that this rich and temperate environment afforded them cedar forests to use for building homes and carving canoes as well as native grasses and mountain goat wool to use for weaving baskets and blankets. They also discovered a bounty of food in the nearby waters where they hunted marine mammals, collected shrimp and other shellfish, and caught salmon. And, of course, they also fished for crabs.

With so many available resources, the people were able to build permanent homes here with hand-hewn wall planks and built-in benches covered with grass mats for sleeping. At the center of each home sat the hearth, a gathering place above which fish were often strung on racks for smoking. They also built longhouses, sometimes encompassing nearly two thousand square feet, where they held festive community events known as potlatches. These gatherings included enormous feasts to celebrate marriages, births, and deaths, along with recognition of social rankings, and they always included a distribution of gifts and sharing of food.

In the mid-eighteenth century, they began to hear stories from other tribes about an impending arrival of people who spoke strange languages, worshipped different deities, and rode in extraordinary water vessels with tall masts. And then, in 1792, a young boy of Duwamish heritage, around six years old at the time, watched the HMS *Discovery* sail into view with British explorer George Vancouver at the helm.

Soon enough, an influx of new people showed up from all around the world. Canadian fur traders came for pelts. Scandinavians came to work in the burgeoning fishing and lumber industries. Settlers crossed American prairies in search of the promised land. Throughout the first half of the nineteenth century, the region experienced numerous skirmishes among the tribes and the newcomers. It was a period of great change—and great disruption.

In 1841, a US naval officer surveyed a large bay in Puget Sound, which he later named Elliott Bay. Its depth was nearly six hundred feet in some areas, and its waters were relatively protected from ferocious storms by the surrounding land topography. In addition, the Duwamish River emptied into the bay, thereby connecting the inland forests to the sound and ultimately the ocean. Elliott Bay was destined to quickly become the anchor of Puget Sound's fishing, shipping, timber, mining, and tourist industries for decades to come.

The first American settlers, arriving in 1851, set up homesteads on land known as Duwamish Head, which was already home to some of the Indigenous people. Historians believe that one of the men the

The USS Decatur, *one of several government ships that were moved to the Puget Sound region in the 1850s, as hostility grew between the Native peoples and the new settlers before the Battle of Seattle.*

settlers encountered had been the young boy watching Vancouver sail into his peoples' waters years earlier. He was now the Duwamish chief Si'ahl, and within several years the new town developed on the other side of the bay would be named after him: Seattle.

In 1854 and 1855, the United States signed treaties with various tribes around the country, including those located in the Puget Sound region. Terms involved payment of cash for land and requirements that the tribes relocate to designated reservations. In exchange, the US government promised that the tribes would be able to retain fishing rights. But many of the tribespeople did not agree with the terms, and the government didn't abide by many of its promises.

The Battle of Seattle erupted in January 1856 near the waterfront. Tribes from throughout the Washington Territory came to participate in the uprising, and some settlers evacuated based on Chief Seattle's advance warnings that trouble was forthcoming. The American military quashed the attack, and over the next few years many of the Native peoples moved to reservations as called for by the Treaty of Point Elliott, but some remained in or near the central waterfront and tried to figure out how to live a new lifestyle and blend into what was becoming a predominantly white community. Chief Seattle was among them, and he built a longhouse at the corner of what is now First Avenue South and South King Street, a short walk from where the piers would later be built.

Meanwhile, the central waterfront of Elliott Bay had been moving forward with development and expansion. Industrialists built a steam-powered sawmill to process enormous logs skidded down the Duwamish River from old-growth forests, and the timber was then shipped from the wharf, often destined for San Francisco. The deep harbor also became a magnet for shipyards, foundries, and banks. By the mid-1870s, the region had nearly exhausted its supply of timber, but coal replaced it as the leading export, transported from regional mines to the waterfront by narrow-gauge railroads. The economy

A lumber mill and pier on tideflats at the waterfront.

fluctuated during the 1880s and 1890s, but overall the population continued to grow at an astounding rate, from 3,553 in 1880 to 42,837 in 1890 and 80,871 by the turn of the century. In addition to the industries centered on the waterfront, the population growth reflected the arrival of gold prospectors, who came stampeding into town during the final years of the century. Many of them set sail from Elliott Bay for the Yukon gold rush in search of the mother lode, giving the city its reputation as the Gateway to Alaska.

By then, numerous warehouses had been built along the water's edge. Although a massive fire ignited in the basement of a local store in 1889, engulfing and destroying much of the city and the early piers, the city was determined to rebuild. As part of that effort, plans called for greater efficiency and capacity by setting the new piers at unique angles. This way, trains wouldn't have to make sharp,

Above: A ship leaves the Seattle waterfront during the Alaska gold rush, 1898. Opposite, top: East Waterway, Lander Street Terminal, 1914. Opposite, bottom: A waterfront fire station with fireboats Snoqualmie *and* Duwamish, *1910. After a massive fire in 1889, Seattle was determined to rebuild.*

right-angle turns upon arrival, and ships would be less likely to collide with each other. The angles also gave the piers more protection from inclement weather. But perhaps most importantly, the new designs would be more economical to build because the angles allowed the piers to be built closer to shore and thus the pilings to be shorter. When the delta at the Duwamish River's mouth was filled in to accommodate the new construction, the new piers—numbered from south to north—served the Alaska Steamship Company, which transported passengers, fishing products, and dogsleds to and from Alaska. It also served as the base for dozens of private transportation vessels known as the Mosquito Fleet, which included numerous cargo ships exporting grain and other materials, and steamships transporting military personnel and dignitaries.

As time went on, the waterfront became increasingly reliant on the area's maritime industry as steamships and ferries transported more and more passengers traveling up and down the West Coast. At the same time, more cargo ships were crossing the Pacific Ocean

for international trade with Japan, China, and the Philippines. The area of the city immediately surrounding the piers also expanded with the development of the historic Pioneer Square and Pike Place Market, a seawall to protect Railroad Avenue from the water, the arrival of military operations during the two world wars, and a facility to serve amphibian planes. Fish storage and processing operations were also a mainstay of the central waterfront district well into the 1950s. But by then the face of the area was beginning to change. Many of the structures had become worn and obsolete, and when the Port of Seattle built a modern, container-friendly terminal south of the central waterfront, the City of Seattle had to make a decision: demolish the old piers or find a better use for them.

Ultimately, because the piers were intricately linked with Seattle's history, and many of their key physical and architectural features were still relatively intact, the city decided to retain them and to shift the focus of the central waterfront toward recreation and tourism.

The 1962 World's Fair, which showcased an ultramodern monorail and the world-renowned Space Needle, prompted the building of a hotel, a large import store, and more restaurants and curio shops along the piers. A waterfront park and the Seattle Aquarium were opened in 1977, and the new cruise terminal for Alaska-bound travelers opened in the 1990s. Then, in 2010, a comprehensive plan to transform the waterfront was initiated to install a promenade with bike lanes, establish parks and beaches, restore marine habitat, and improve access to the waterfront from downtown. In 2023, the City of Seattle honorarily named Elliott Way, the street that runs alongside the waterfront, Dzidzilalich, which means "little crossing-over place" in the Coast Salish Lushootseed language, to acknowledge that the waterfront sits on the land and shared waters of the Coast Salish people.

Waterfront construction at Railroad Avenue, north and south of Broad Street, 1934.

Miners Landing and the Crab Pot Restaurant

One of the chief contributors to the transformation of the central waterfront district was Hal Griffith, the founder of the Crab Pot Restaurant and Miners Landing.

Hal's love of the water, his entrepreneurial skills, and his interest in seafood were sparked at an early age. As a young boy growing up in Gig Harbor, Washington, he sold popcorn and apples to cars waiting in line at the Tacoma Narrows ferry. In high school, he played on the basketball team and ran the concession stand during halftime. As a young adult, when he was invited to manage a local restaurant, he learned the ins and outs of the restaurant industry. Eventually, Hal found his way to Seattle's waterfront, where he set up a fish-and-chips stand and, later, a self-serve fish-smoking stand named the Salmon Cooker Restaurant, which served Pacific Northwest salmon, halibut, and cod cooked over an open alderwood flame. He also opened an import shop he called Pirate's Plunder, remodeled the front of the building, and restored some of the interior while retaining the original walls and timbers. As the founder and president of a community association, Hal advocated for renovation of the area while also preserving the piers as historic reminders of Seattle's heritage.

Years later, after Hal became a father, he was eager to introduce his kids to the water and the boating life, frequently taking them out to fish for salmon, catch crabs, or dig for clams or oysters. As his son Kyle puts it, they were all "born and raised Seattle." They would often coordinate their days with other families, with some fishing for salmon while others would dig for shellfish. At the end of the day, the families would meet and tie their boats together, spread out their fresh catches on sheets of newspaper, and share the feast with one another.

This communal sharing of seafood riches ultimately became the inspiration for the Crab Pot Restaurant, which opened in 1992, and its signature dish: the Seafeast. A collection of seafood heaped from giant buckets right onto the butcher-paper-lined table, it's an experience for everyone, from inquisitive young diners to the young at heart, all wielding wooden mallets to crack shells and relishing the delicious mess of it all.

Today's menu at the Crab Pot Restaurant features a variety of Seafeast combinations that rely on time-honored cooking methods to preserve and enhance the flavors and textures. The simplest medley is the Cove, featuring steamed clams, mussels, and head-on shrimp served with andouille sausage, corn on the cob, and red potatoes and seasoned with the restaurant's signature Seaspice. Another combination is the Alaskan; in addition to what is included in the Cove, this dish includes jumbo and regular snow crab and Dungeness crab. The Clam Bake is also a favorite, featuring a salmon skewer in lieu of the jumbo snow crab. But the menu offers so much more, including coconut prawns, oyster shooters, grilled wild salmon or halibut, crab macaroni and cheese, fish and chips, tacos, and salads. The Crab Pot Restaurant serves up astounding flavor with a focus on fresh, wild, and local seafood when practical, depending on what's in season and available.

The restaurant's family-friendly environment has been a hit along the waterfront for years. But Hal's entrepreneurial vision didn't stop there. He went on to further develop Pier 57 into an even more vibrant entertainment hub, and he purchased the pier in its entirety in 1989. He named it Miners Landing and remained committed to honoring the rich-yet-rustic history of the waterfront, embracing its historical significance to the Alaska gold rush even though modern buildings and storefronts were popping up all around him. According to Kyle, tradition has always been more important to Hal than the ultramodern lifestyle, and this was recognized in 2007

when the pier received a distinction as a Seattle Landmark by the city's Landmarks Preservation Board.

In addition to the Crab Pot Restaurant and the Salmon Cooker Restaurant, today's visitors can dine on the pier at the Alaskan Sourdough Bakery or the Fisherman's Restaurant. They can marvel at old sepia photos, animal heads, and wood-carved Duwamish art installations. They can play at the arcade or relive their youth riding an old-fashioned carousel or soar above the pier on the Seattle Great Wheel, which opened in 2012. Rising 175 feet into the sky, it makes three full revolutions for each rider and displays nighttime LED light shows to celebrate home football games or holidays. Another Miners Landing attraction is the aerial adventure Wings over Washington: A Flying Ride, which uses state-of-the-art technology to take guests on a virtual tour around Washington State to visit national parks, waterfalls, and even a balloon stampede. Guests can also embark on the *Orca I* or *Orca II* for a Salish Sea boat tour, which showcases the sights of Elliott Bay while offering passengers a full bar, salmon meals, and more. It also introduces guests to the history of the Duwamish in the region. And perhaps best of all, the pier offers stunning views of Elliott Bay in the shadow of the Seattle skyline. If you're lucky, you might even spot a pod of the Southern Resident orcas breaching, bellyflopping, or spy hopping. And although you won't see it, you can be sure that, beneath the surface of the shimmering blue water, the giant Pacific octopus waits for nightfall so it can hunt for its own meal of Dungeness crab and head-on shrimp.

When asked how he envisions the future of Miners Landing and the Crab Pot Restaurant, Kyle says the culture will always remain uniquely Pacific Northwest, and the main mission is to continue to create an affordable experience for everyone to come and enjoy.

The recipes in this cookbook are inspired by the Crab Pot Restaurant menu, with each dish scaled and made easier for you, the home cook. Of course, these recipes aren't a substitute for the full sensory experience on the waterfront at the Crab Pot!

Pantry and Equipment

Want to be ready to go whenever a Crab Pot craving arises? This section covers all the special ingredients—and special equipment—needed to re-create the yummy meals at the restaurant. You may already have the bulk of these items in your pantry, but even if some are unfamiliar, most are easily found at the grocery store.

THE CRAB POT SEAFOOD SPICE

This is the Crab Pot's secret *sauce*. With over a dozen ingredients, Seaspice flavors all of the Seafeasts, shrimp tacos, and so much more. When you're cooking at home, substitute with any seafood spice.

THE SAUCES

Tabasco Red Pepper Sauce and Tabasco Green Pepper Sauce

You are likely familiar with the classic red pepper Tabasco sauce in the tiny bottle, but did you know that Tabasco also comes in *green*? Choose it whenever you want a hit of jalapeño flavor.

Tapatio Hot Sauce

The Crab Pot's go-to hot sauce carries slightly more heat than its American neighbor Tabasco. Fun fact: the company name Tapatio refers to a person who hails from Guadalajara, in Mexico, where hot sauce is king.

Sweet Chili Sauce

Simultaneously sweet and savory, tangy and spicy, sweet chili sauce is made from a combination of red chili, vinegar, garlic, and—depending on which brand you choose—sweetened with sugar or honey.

Horseradish Sauce

Horseradish sauce is a grated-up version of the spicy root vegetable that hails from the mustard family. Made with vinegar and salt, it's a creamy concoction with a distinctive kick that hits somewhere between spicy brown mustard and wasabi.

Worcestershire Sauce

Named for the city from which it comes, Worcester, and the English term for *county*, "shire," this sauce's complex flavor (sweet plus salty plus savory) is so much easier to use than it is to pronounce.

Mayonnaise

At its core mayonnaise is just eggs and oil, but this common condiment is what takes many of the Crab Pot recipes a long way into their distinctive creamy flavor.

SOME CLAM–SPECIFIC FLAVORINGS

Clamato Juice

Clamato is the brand name for the clam-plus-tomato juice that's easily found with other juices at most grocery stores. It's not only good to have at the ready for **Tomato Herb Aioli** (page 155), but also makes a great mixer. Combined with vodka, it's part of the drink called a Caesar, similar to the more well-known Bloody Mary.

Clam Juice

Nature's bouillon, clam juice is a broth made from steaming in-the-shell clams—often without any added spices. Not only does it flavor a slew of seafood dishes, it is also drunk solo and is the *clam* ingredient in Clamato juice.

Clam Base

Think of clam base as you would tomato paste. It's a similar

consistency and essentially the *essence* of clams (clam flavor plus salt). Used solo or in conjunction with clam juice, clam base is a key ingredient in the Crab Pot's chowders. If it isn't available at your local market, substitute with chicken or beef bouillon base. The result won't be quite the same, but it will add some flavor.

AND THEN SOME

Panko

Panko is simply Japanese breadcrumbs—*pan* means "bread" and *ko* means "crumbs" or "powder." Made from steamed crustless loaves, the result is a flakier crumb that provides a crispier finish than regular breadcrumbs. You can purchase panko seasoned or unseasoned, but the Crab Pot chefs prefer the latter, adding their seasoning of choice to the mix.

Granulated Garlic

The only difference between granulated garlic and the more commonly known garlic powder is the size of the grain. Both items are made from ground dried garlic. Garlic powder has a flour-like consistency that easily incorporates into a recipe. The coarse sand-like texture of granulated garlic retains a slightly crunchy finish.

OUR GO-TO DRIED SPICES

- Basil
- Bay leaves
- Cayenne pepper
- Celery salt
- Cumin
- Dill weed
- Onion powder
- Oregano
- Paprika
- Parsley
- Thyme

FRESH ITEMS (NOT SHELF-STABLE)

Minced Garlic

If you aren't a stickler for fresh-from-the-clove garlic, a ready-to-go jar of minced garlic (available in water or oil) kept in the fridge will save you from the mess and trouble of peeling and mincing.

Lemons or Lemon Juice

Lemons are ubiquitous with seafood cooking—and eating. You will thank yourself for keeping fresh lemons or lemon juice from concentrate in the fridge and on your rolling grocery list.

> **TIP!** No lemons, no problem. Here are a few items that will do in a pinch in a 1:1 ratio: lime juice, orange juice, vinegar, white wine, or lemon zest.

Parmesan Cheese

This hard cheese made from cow's milk is sweet and nutty by itself but is often blended with its salty, sharp sheep-based partner Romano in a 75-to-25 mix. For some dishes, like the **Pier 57 Smoked Salmon Fettucine** (page 131), the cheeses prove better together. Choose bags of pre-shredded Parmesan for the easiest recipe prep.

SPECIAL EQUIPMENT

Bibs

The Crab Pot has signature bibs, which are a good idea to wear while eating crabs at home too. When napkins can't keep up with the action, strap on a bib and eat with abandon.

Butcher Paper

To serve Seafeasts like the Crab Pot does, keep a roll of brown paper in the kitchen. It makes cleanup much easier!

Crab Cracker or Mallet

Crab crackers or mallets are used to break into sections of the crab legs to get to the meat. Crab crackers are easier to clean than mallets and are easier to store in a home drawer. Essential for Seafeasts.

Steamer Pot

Also known as a crab pot, the two-part steaming pot includes a large pot with a steamer insert and is critical to steaming seafood.

Deep Fryer

For some of the Crab Pot's deep-fried dishes, this cookbook provides simpler directions for searing the meal.

Fish Spatula

This long, thin spatula slips under delicate fish, simplifying the flip-and-turn process.

Fresh Fish Buying Guide

The Crab Pot uses fresh-caught seafood whenever it is available—and you can too. No matter the particulars on how to recognize a fresh fish, crustacean, or bivalve, a general indicator with any seafood meat purchase is its smell. Seek out ingredients with a clean, ocean-like aroma. Avoid a strong *fishy* one. For specifics on all the seafood meat ingredients that appear in the Crab Pot recipes, keep reading.

FISH

Salmon

For the freshest salmon, make sure that you purchase your fish from a reputable market. The Crab Pot recommends king salmon as the premier salmon. If king salmon is unavailable or out of your price range, choose coho or sockeye as a high-quality alternative.

Halibut

Halibut is a lean white fish known for its thick and meaty texture. It is sold whole or as a fillet or steak. If you are purchasing a whole fish, look for one that has clear eyes.

If purchasing pre-cut, choose one with a glossy white translucency to the flesh, avoiding anything that looks dull or yellow. If purchased frozen, halibut does a good job of retaining its moisture.

Calamari (Squid)

Technically a mollusk, not a fish, calamari is a type of squid. Available fresh or frozen, calamari meat is made up of bodies (tubes) and tentacles. If you are able to find fresh squid, choose ones with clear eyes and moist flesh. If the frozen food section is your destination, the world is your oyster with whole and cut sections of calamari, including steaks.

TIP! Be sure to check your recipe before purchasing. The **Breaded Calamari** appetizer (page 78) requires calamari *steaks* (fresh or frozen), which are large flat pieces of meat from large squids as opposed to the more common mixed bag o' tubes and tentacles.

CRUSTACEANS

Crab

You can purchase crab pre-cooked or still alive. When choosing a whole cooked crab, look for one with a firm shell that feels heavy for its size. Curled legs are another good indicator; it means the crab was cooked alive, so it will hold up better in the cooking process and taste better. If you are buying a live crab, choose a *lively* one. Quick and alert is a sign of good health and good taste.

TIP! Dungeness crabs are named for the narrow stretch of northwest Washington State called the Dungeness Spit—a fertile and sandy habitat where this species is primarily harvested.

Shrimp

Head-on shrimp, or shrimp sold in their shell, tend to be the most flavorful of your options. If you prefer an easier eating process, you can purchase ready-to-cook shrimp shelled with heads removed and deveined. Ready-to-cook—or cooked and ready to eat—shrimp come in several sizes, bay shrimp being the smallest.

BIVALVES

Keep safe and carry on: all bivalves (clams, mussels, and oysters) must be purchased alive with their hard shells tightly closed.

Clams

Clams must be purchased alive with their hard shells tightly closed. If they are slightly open or you are unsure about one, tap it with your finger. If it closes up, the clam is alive and safe to eat/cook. If it doesn't close or is cracked or broken, do not use it. Also, don't eat any clam that remains closed after the cooking process.

Mussels

Mussels must be purchased alive with their hard shells tightly closed, although a tiny sliver open is OK. To test, press the shell closed. If it stays shut, the mussel is alive and safe to eat/cook. If it reopens, discard the mussel. Also, don't eat any mussel that remains closed after the cooking process. Farm-raised mussels tend to have less grit than wild mussels and usually come debearded for easier prep.

Oysters

Oysters must be purchased alive with their hard shells tightly closed. Look for ones on ice at the market. They should feel heavy for their size, which indicates they are full of their natural juice, referred to as liquor, literally their life juice. Skip any with open shells or ones that sound hollow when tapped. In the fridge, keep them flat or stored in a bowl covered with a wet paper towel to help prevent their juices from leaking out till you are ready to shuck them.

> **TIP!** Fish fact: oysters and crabs get their specific name—and taste—from the very body of water they're harvested from.

How to Pick a Crab

With a cooked crab in front of you . . .

1. Flip the crab over and use a knife to remove the triangular bit called the apron. After you remove the apron, place your thumbs between the front and back of the crab and pry open the carapace (top lid of the crab).
2. Scrape out the spongy, inedible gills on both sides of the crab body, and remove the rest of the loose innards. Do not be alarmed by the brown "mustard." Discard everything you've removed.
3. Break the crab in half using your hands. (For tougher shells, you might need the help of a knife.)
4. Twist and pull off each crab leg, using a crab cracker if needed.
5. With that same crab cracker, crack the two main crab claws using light force so you don't shatter the shell and with it all the crabmeat. You can also hit the claws with a mallet for this step.
6. Using a small fork or your hands, remove all the meat from the claws.
7. Using a crab cracker or kitchen scissors, cut open each crab leg to reveal a solid piece of crabmeat.
8. Using a small fork or your hands, pick out the meat from the body.

> **TIP!** Start with the claws for the sweetest meat. And don't be surprised at the ratio of shell to meat—only about 25 percent of a crab's body weight yields edible meat.

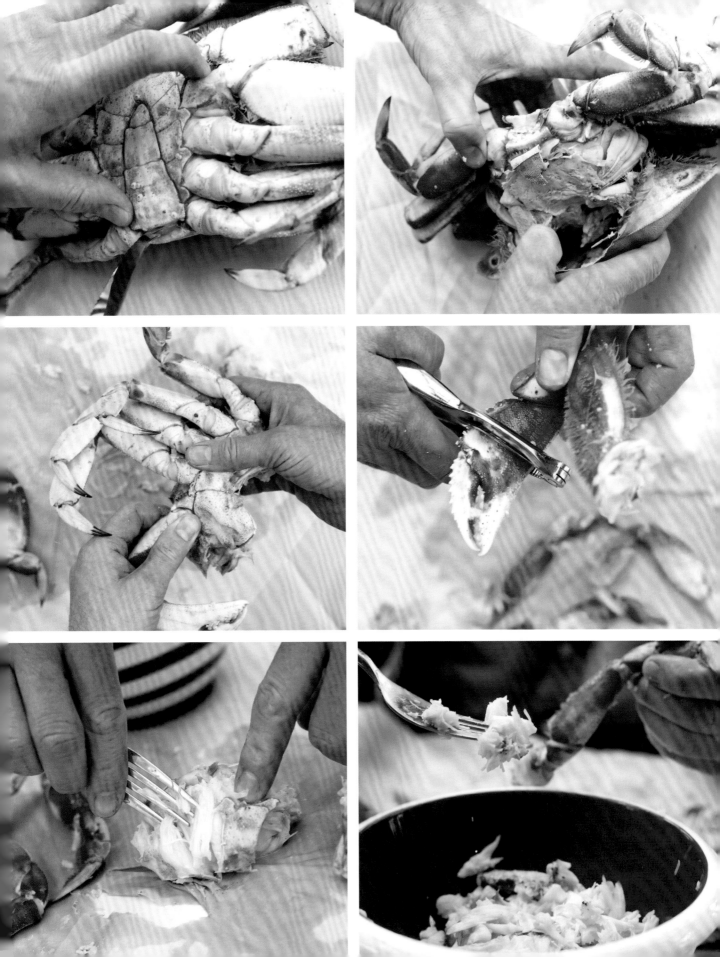

The Seafeast

THE SEAFEAST METHOD

Makes enough for 2 hungry,
adventurous eaters

The Alaskan Seafeast

16 ounces jumbo opilio crab
sections
14 ounces clams, scrubbed and
rinsed
12 ounces mussels, scrubbed and
rinsed
10 ounces head-on shrimp
8 ounces Dungeness crab sections
8 ounces snow crab sections
8 ounces salmon chunks on
skewers
6 oysters on the half shell
12 medium-sized red potatoes, cut
in half crosswise
2 ears of corn, quartered
4 ounces andouille sausage, angle-
sliced
2 tablespoons Crab Pot Seaspice
or alternate seafood seasoning

Special equipment:

Steamer pot
Oyster knife (optional)
Bamboo skewers
Butcher paper
Crab cracker or mallet
Bibs

Seafeasts are a mélange of seafood, steamed with mouthwatering spices, corn, potatoes—and sometimes sausage—but always poured onto butcher paper and enjoyed with one's hands. Bibs. Mallets. Go for it! This recipe takes you through the big kahuna version called the Alaskan. This recipe calls for jumbo opilio, Dungeness, and snow crab, but you can use any crab of your choice. Once you've mastered this one, you'll be ready for any of the Crab Pot's tried-and-true combos in this section.

In a steamer pot over medium-high heat, fill the bottom with water (no salt needed) and bring to a boil. Line your eating surface with butcher paper, and set out mallets and bibs.

Meanwhile, into an extra-large bowl, add all your desired ingredients. Shake the Seaspice on top of everything, and mix well. Pour into the top part of the steamer pot, and steam for about 8 to 10 minutes. When the clams are open and the shrimp is white, your Seafeast is ready to eat. Pour it out onto the butcher paper, and enjoy.

THE PARTS OF A SEAFEAST

Crab

For the sake of the Seafeast, all crabs are pre-cooked and cut in half for easy mix-and-matching. Just note quantities and feel free to substitute one for another. See **A Crab Primer** (page 52) to study the differences.

Clams

Examine your clams by checking that all clam shells are tightly closed with no broken bits. Dispose of any less-than-stellar clams. Then with a stiff brush, scrub and rinse the shells under cold running water to remove any debris. Now they are ready to add to the feast.

Mussels

Be sure that all of your mussels are tightly closed with the shells intact (no broken pieces). Discard any that don't match this description. Then with a stiff brush, scrub and rinse mussel shells under cold running water to remove beards and any leftover debris before adding ready-to-go mussels to the feast.

Oysters

Are your oyster shells closed tight? If the answer is yes, scrub and rinse the shells, keeping them level so you don't lose any of their liquor. Shuck them open and set aside the half shells until ready for use.

How to shuck: Hold the oyster against a cloth on a hard surface with the flat part facing up. Using an oyster knife, pry the shell open and cut completely toward the opposite side, removing the top flat shell. Then cut the oyster free from the bottom shell using the same knife.

Head-On Shrimp

These will go into the mix with the head and shell intact. No need to remove them in advance. The shrimp will cook in their "coats," and be sweeter for it. Be prepared to remove them during the eating process instead.

Red Potatoes

Red potatoes are low-starch, high-moisture potatoes that hold their shape well. You'll want medium-sized specimens unpeeled and cut in half cross-wise (not lengthwise) for large chunky bits that will soften but not get mushy in the cooking process.

Corn

Remove the husk and silk using this tricky method: from the stalk end, cut off the top couple of inches. Repeat with each ear. Place the corn on a plate and microwave for 2 to 4 minutes. While holding on to the uncut end of each ear, perform a shake and squeeze motion and watch the corncob slide out. Cut each ear crosswise into four equal parts. If using pre-husked and pre-silked corn on the cob, simply jump to the step where you cut each ear crosswise into four equal parts.

Sausage

Andouille is a pork sausage and the Crab Pot's choice for Seafeasts because of its chunky texture and smoky flavor. Slice each sausage into 1-inch angles. (Most pre-made sausages are about 3 ounces, so you'll need more than one for each Seafeast.)

Salmon Skewers

Using your choice of salmon steak, cut four (1-ounce) chunks and pierce them onto a skewer. This way they won't break up and get lost in the feast.

The Seafeast 49

> **TIP!** For guidelines on how to purchase the freshest of fresh seafood to use in any of the Crab Pot's Seafeasts, please first read the **Fresh Fish Buying Guide** (page 38).

CUSTOMIZE YOUR SEAFEAST

Using the same method for the **Alaskan Seafeast** (page 46), re-create any of the Crab Pot's menu-item Seafeasts, or get creative mixing and matching your favorite ingredients.

King Crab Seafeast

2 pounds king crab sections
12 medium-sized red potatoes, cut in half crosswise
2 ears of corn, quartered
2 tablespoons Crab Pot Seaspice or alternate seafood seasoning

Bairdi Crab Seafeast

2 pounds Bairdi crab sections
12 medium-sized red potatoes, cut in half crosswise
2 ears of corn, quartered
2 tablespoons Crab Pot Seaspice or alternate seafood seasoning

The Cove

12 ounces clams, scrubbed and rinsed
10 ounces mussels, scrubbed and rinsed
8 ounces head-on shrimp
8 medium-sized red potatoes, cut in half crosswise
1 ear of corn, quartered
4 ounces andouille sausage, angle-sliced
2 tablespoons Crab Pot Seaspice or alternate seafood seasoning

The Pacific

20 ounces Dungeness crab sections
12 ounces clams, scrubbed and rinsed
10 ounces mussels, scrubbed and rinsed
8 ounces head-on shrimp
12 medium-sized red potatoes, cut in half crosswise
2 ears of corn, quartered
4 ounces andouille sausage, angle-sliced
2 tablespoons Crab Pot Seaspice or alternate seafood seasoning

The Westport

14 ounces clams, scrubbed and rinsed
12 ounces mussels, scrubbed and rinsed
10 ounces head-on shrimp
8 ounces snow crab sections
8 ounces Dungeness crab sections
12 medium-sized red potatoes, cut in half crosswise
2 ears of corn, quartered
4 ounces andouille sausage, angle-sliced
2 tablespoons Crab Pot Seaspice or alternate seafood seasoning

Clam Bake

To make the **Clam Bake**, add to the **Westport**:
8 ounces salmon chunks on skewers
6 oysters on the half shell

Crab and Shrimp

1 pound Dungeness crab sections
1 pound snow crab sections
1 pound head-on shrimp
12 medium-sized red potatoes, cut in half crosswise
2 ears of corn, quartered
2 tablespoons Crab Pot Seaspice or alternate seafood seasoning

Crab and Salmon

1 pound Dungeness crab sections
1 pound snow crab sections
1 pound salmon chunks on skewers
12 medium-sized red potatoes, cut in half crosswise
2 ears of corn, quartered
2 tablespoons Crab Pot Seaspice or alternate seafood seasoning

Snow and Dungeness Crab

1 pound Dungeness crab sections
1 pound snow crab sections
12 medium-sized red potatoes, cut in half crosswise
2 ears of corn, quartered
2 tablespoons Crab Pot Seaspice or alternate seafood seasoning

A Crab Primer

The Pacific Northwest waters teem with diverse and abundant marine life, and to the Coast Salish and other Indigenous peoples of the region, the food fished and gathered from the Salish Sea has long been a vital source of nutrition to be treated with care, respect, and gratitude. Nearly three hundred foods have been identified as historically important to their diets, and the many varieties of seafood available in this region are high on that list. This includes shellfish, which refers to seafaring invertebrates that breathe through gills and generally don't have fins, and finfish, which refers to aquatic animals with gills and backbones that *do* have fins. Shellfish are often categorized as either crustaceans, which have hard outer shells and segmented limbs like crabs and shrimp, or mollusks, whose soft bodies are contained completely inside their shells, such as clams and oysters.

CRAB FISHING: THEN AND NOW

Crabs live in intertidal zones along the coastline. Their diverse microhabitats are constantly changing as tides come and go, and the resilience and adaptability of the regional species have allowed them to survive within our changing environment. Crabs are well suited to challenging aquatic and meteorological conditions because they are able to seek out and burrow into rocks, sand, or any other good hiding places—and they can defend themselves with the hard, armor-like shells on their backs, known as carapaces, and their dangerous pincer claws.

Some live directly on the shoreline, while others venture farther out into deeper waters, depending on their species and life cycle stage. They generally live on the seafloor, sometimes hundreds of feet below the surface, where the water is colder and they are better hidden from land animals and hungry predatory birds. Like other

arthropods, crabs are covered by an exoskeleton to protect their soft bodies, which must be periodically molted so the crab can grow.

Historically, Indigenous women of the region collected crabs at low tide, among the eelgrass waving in shallow waters. Men often hunted them near the shoreline on foot or from canoes using spears designed to daze the crabs and pierce their shells. They also caught crabs using cages or stone-weighted lines lowered into the water from canoes.

After European explorers arrived with new fishing, processing, and storing methods, the commercial crab-fishing industry took off. By the mid-1880s, Dungeness crabs were being fished along the West Coast using trotlines, tangle nets, and otter trawls—methods that maximized efficiency and harvest but that, unfortunately, also often indiscriminately caught a myriad of other sea life, including immature and female crabs. Crab canneries also began to pop up and were a game changer because crabmeat no longer needed to be eaten fresh.

The crab pot, patented in the 1920s, was designed to sit on the seafloor and lure crabs into the trap through tunnels that the crabs were unable to escape through. First constructed of wood, salmon trap wire, and netting, the pots weren't durable and had to be replaced every year. But even so they revolutionized the industry because they could lure and catch a lot of crabs at once, and the crabs would remain alive, with the pot attached to a buoy floating in cold water, until the fishermen could return to retrieve them. Any crabs that needed to be released would be unharmed using this fishing method. By the 1960s, crab pot frames were made from steel, and the netting from stainless steel, which meant they could be used over and over again for multiple seasons. This style of crab pot, still used today, allows caught crabs to move about while in the trap and includes escape rings for small crabs.

Although crabs had been fished for decades, the domestic commercial crab industry really found its footing in Alaska after

World War II, when technological advancements made it possible for long-distance fishing and processing vessels to stay out at sea for months with little oversight or regulation. Even after some regulations were introduced in the 1960s, after Alaska became a state, the bountiful harvests of Alaskan king and snow crabs remained reminiscent of Alaska's gold rush in the previous century. The seemingly infinite supply of crab, later attributed to years of unusually cold conditions that were perfect for crab larvae, led fishermen from around the world to descend on Alaska. Some reported annual earnings of $100,000 back in the mid-twentieth century, and dozens of crab canneries popped up near the Alaskan coastline. Old-timers came to resent the influx of opportunistic fishermen, much as the Indigenous people surely felt when the Europeans first arrived and disrupted their fisheries. In the 1980s, the Alaskan crab industry took a nosedive. Harvests plummeted, canneries closed, and bankruptcies followed.

Biologists have theorized that water conditions shifted and grew warmer, creating the perfect conditions for diseases that the crabs couldn't ward off. In the decades since then, state and federal agencies have established strict regulations surrounding commercial and recreational crab fishing in Alaska and in the Lower 48, with limits on how many can be caught and when (or whether) the season opens, depending in part on the size and health of any particular fishery's crab population in any given year, as well as other factors including the presence of algae toxins. The season can also be different for commercial, tribal, and recreational fishermen.

Millions of pounds of Dungeness crabs are normally harvested each year along the Pacific coast, with most processed and frozen. Unfortunately, the southern part of Puget Sound has experienced population issues for years with full-season closures. Given that crab fishing makes a significant contribution to the local communities in terms of both revenues and employment opportunities, such closures can be extremely disappointing, and costly, for everyone.

DUNGENESS CRAB

The Dungeness crab (*Metacarcinus magister*) can be found from Alaska to Mexico, but historically it has thrived in abundance in Puget Sound, particularly in the north sound and near Seattle. The crab derives its common name from one of its favorite habitats near the town of Dungeness on Washington's Olympic Peninsula.

The Dungeness crab has an oval hard shell for its carapace, or back, that is covered with spines, and a white apron on its underside. Its shell can range in color from yellow to purple to brown, while its legs are usually a deep red or orange. It has serrated pincer claws that appear to have white gloves on their tips. Normally six or seven inches in diameter across the back, some Dungeness crabs can grow to ten inches if they achieve their full life expectancy of about ten years.

These crabs start out in larval form when they're hatched and spend the first several months of life suspended in water, swept out to sea or back toward the shore at the whim of the water's currents. Once they reach the juvenile stage, they burrow in shallow coastal waters, among pilings, or in beds of eelgrass, where the saline content is low. There, they feed on small fish, clams, shrimp, and other crustaceans while trying to avoid being eaten by other marine predators, including adult crabs. They molt up to six times per year while young, exposing their soft, greenish bodies until the new shells harden. When they reach adulthood, Dungeness crabs along the Pacific Coast might live in depths of up to five hundred or six hundred feet and feed on a variety of fish, clams, and other crustaceans using their sharp teeth. As adults, they still molt annually in unison with other crabs, and they mate just after molting.

ALASKAN KING CRAB

The Alaskan king crab (*Paralithodes camtschaticus*) makes its home in the Bering Sea, among the Alaskan Aleutian Islands, and along the coast of British Columbia. Because it requires the coldest of waters to survive, this crab embodies Alaska's rugged image. Fishing for Alaskan king crabs can be even more dangerous than fishing for Dungeness crabs, especially because the season coincides with some of the coldest months of the year, from October or November and into January, when a fisherman's accidental plunge into the waters can mean nearly immediate death. Even a splash of the frigid water on exposed skin can cause painful lesions.

Also known as the red king crab, this behemoth can weigh up to twenty pounds or more, with an adult's leg span reaching five or six feet. Its shiny, thick shell ranges in color from brownish orange to deep red, and it can measure up to eleven inches across the back. Its pincer claws are asymmetrical, with one claw used for crushing prey and the other for eating delicate foods, and it only uses three pairs of legs for walking; the fourth pair remains tucked under the carapace and is used only for reproductive purposes.

When eggs are released, Alaskan king crab larvae drift in the water until they're several months old. Although still no larger than a dime at that point, they burrow on the seafloor among algae and other protective habitats to avoid being eaten by octopuses, sea otters, and other crabs. Young red king crabs will eat whatever they can catch, preferring algae, worms, and small clams or other animals. As they grow older, they form large pods for protection against predators—sometimes thousands of crabs all together—as they move about on the ocean floor. Mature Alaskan king crabs use their strong claws to crush and devour other crabs, sea stars, fish, sand dollars, and whatever dead or decaying animals they find. As adults, they have few predators, especially when traveling in large groups, and they can live twenty years or more if not first caught by a crab fisherman. Given that they must be at least seven inches in diameter and weigh seven and a half pounds in order to be harvested, they are generally seven to nine years old if they are caught.

SNOW CRAB

There are two primary species of snow crabs harvested in Alaska: the true snow crab that the Crab Pot uses on its menu (*Chionoecetes opilio*) and the southern Tanner crab (*Chionoecetes bairdi*), often compared to the Alaskan king crab because of its stronger flavor profile. These two distinct species have been known to crossbreed in the wild. Both species of snow crab can be found around the globe in cold northern waters, and most of the snow crabs found on menus or in seafood counters in the Pacific Northwest come from the eastern Bering Sea in Alaska.

Also known as a spider crab, the snow crab is shaped like a spider and is normally tinged with muted shades of orange and brown. It has four pairs of long, skinny and spiny walking legs, and as it ambles around in muddy or sandy waters, it views its world with green or green-blue eyes. Males are generally about six inches in diameter, whereas females are a petite three inches across. True snow crab males weigh one to two pounds when caught, whereas the Tanners weigh two to four pounds.

The female snow crab releases tens of thousands of eggs, and the hatched larvae feed on phytoplankton or zooplankton before settling onto the soft, sandy ocean floor after a couple of months. There, in the cold, deep water, they burrow for protection and forage for just about anything they deem edible: live fish, shellfish, worms, algae, snails, and sponges, as well as scavenged carcasses. Large marine mammals like seals and otters hunt them, as do octopuses, halibut, and other crabs. Once they reach sexual maturity, they molt one last time, and if they avoid predation, they can live up to twenty years.

Starters

CRAB CAKES WITH JALAPEÑO MARMALADE

Makes about 12 (2½-inch) crab cakes

For the marmalade:

⅔ cup orange marmalade
1½ teaspoons green jalapeño Tabasco sauce
1½ teaspoons chopped fresh cilantro
1 teaspoon lemon juice
Kosher salt
Freshly ground black pepper
Cabbage wedge, for serving (optional)

For the crab cakes:

1 egg
1½ cups panko, divided
¾ cup mayonnaise
½ cup corn (from about ½ ear of corn, knifed off)
½ cup chopped fresh basil
4 green onions, finely chopped
16 ounces lump crabmeat
1 cup canola oil
Chopped red peppers, for garnish
Chopped green onions, for garnish
Cilantro sprigs, for serving
Lemon wedges, for serving

Special equipment:

2½ × 1½-inch biscuit cutter (optional)

Some people make the trek to Pier 57 in Seattle exclusively for the Crab Pot's house specialty: the world's best crab cakes. At the restaurant the chefs deep-fry them, but searing and then finishing them in the oven creates a just as tasty—not to mention healthier—result. They are worth every moment it takes to make them (prep takes about thirty minutes, and total cooking time is about eighteen minutes). The Crab Pot chefs love Dungeness crab, but any combination of crabmeat will work in this recipe as long as it equals one pound total. Serve with spicy jalapeño marmalade as an appetizer or a small-plate meal. If you prefer a sweeter dipping sauce, add a tablespoon of honey to the mix.

———————————

To make the jalapeño marmalade, in a medium bowl, stir together the orange marmalade, green Tabasco, cilantro, and lemon juice until blended. Season to taste with salt and pepper. Set aside.

To make the crab cakes, preheat the oven to 350° F. Line a baking sheet with parchment paper or foil.

Prepare the dipping bowls. In a small bowl, whisk the egg, and set aside. In another small bowl, measure out ¾ cup of panko, and set aside.

In a large bowl, stir together the mayonnaise, corn, basil, and green onions. Add all of the crabmeat and the remaining ¾ cup of panko. Mix by hand until well combined. Using a ¼-cup measuring cup, scoop out and form golf ball–sized balls of the crab mixture by rolling in your hands.

Dip each ball into the egg mixture followed by the bowl of panko, making sure each ball is well covered. Then form each ball into a small hockey-puck shape. (The Crab Pot uses a biscuit cutter for consistency, but hand-formed pucks will work just as well.) Place each puck onto the baking sheet, leaving room in between them so they don't stick together.

In a large skillet over medium-high heat, heat the oil until it's hot and smoky. Sear the crab cakes, cooking each side until nice and brown, about 5 minutes per side, turning once. Note: Be sure not to crowd the crab cakes during the searing process. If you need to, sear them in batches.

As you work, return the cooked crab cakes to the prepared baking sheet. Once all the crab cakes are seared, place them in the oven for about 8 minutes or until the sides are firm to cook fully. Remove from the oven and place them on a paper towel–lined plate to soak up the excess oil.

Sprinkle with red peppers and green onions, and serve two each immediately with a sprig of cilantro and lemon wedge alongside a cabbage triangle filled with jalapeño marmalade.

NOTE: *The Crab Pot serves sauces in a triangle of red cabbage.*

THE CRAB POT CRAB DIP

Makes about 2 cups

12 ounces cream cheese
5 ounces Dungeness crabmeat
2 ounces bay shrimp
2 artichoke hearts
1½ tablespoons shredded
    Parmesan cheese
1½ tablespoons lemon juice
1 teaspoon minced garlic
Dash of Tabasco sauce
Chopped green onions, for garnish
Parsley sprig, for serving
Lemon wedge, for serving
Tortilla chips, for serving

The artichoke pieces will break up as you blend these ingredients together, but they will remain chunky enough to give this savory dip a consistency tailor-made for eating with tortilla chips.

———————————

Preheat the oven to 350° F.

In a large bowl, mix together the cream cheese, crab, shrimp, artichoke, Parmesan, lemon juice, garlic, and Tabasco until just blended, with the hearts broken up but still chunky. Transfer the mixture to a baking dish and bake for 15 minutes, or until just browning on top.

Sprinkle with the green onions. Serve warm with a sprig of parsley and a lemon wedge alongside handfuls of tortilla chips.

CRAB-STUFFED MUSHROOMS

The creamy goodness stuffed inside these mushrooms is similar to the Crab Pot's crab dip, just minus the artichoke hearts. If you like one, you will certainly like the other. This recipe makes an appetizer, but easily scales up to make it a meal for more.

Preheat the oven to 350° F.

For the filling, in a medium bowl, measure out the cream cheese, crab, shrimp, Parmesan, garlic, Tabasco, and lemon juice, and mix by hand. Season to taste with salt.

On a baking sheet, arrange the mushrooms, cap side down. Spoon in the prepared filling, dispersing evenly across the caps. Sprinkle the tops with the ⅔ cup Parmesan. Bake in the oven for 12 minutes.

Remove from the oven, and sprinkle with the green onions. Serve at once with parsley and lemon wedges.

Makes 16 bite-sized stuffed mushrooms

For the filling:

1 cup cream cheese
4 ounces Dungeness crabmeat
2 ounces bay shrimp
2 tablespoons shredded Parmesan cheese
1 teaspoon minced garlic
1 teaspoon Tabasco sauce
1 teaspoon lemon juice
Kosher salt

For the mushrooms:

16 medium-sized button mushrooms, stems removed
⅔ cup shredded Parmesan cheese
Chopped greens onions, for garnish
Parsley sprigs, for serving
Lemon wedges, for serving

OYSTERS ROCKEFELLER

Makes 12 oysters

3 slices bacon
1 tablespoon bacon grease
3 tablespoons minced garlic
6 cups spinach leaves
⅓ cup heavy cream
¼ cup shredded Parmesan cheese
¼ cup cream cheese
½ teaspoon salt
¼ teaspoon ground black pepper
12 fresh oysters on the half shell
Chopped green onions, for garnish
Parsley sprigs, for serving
Lemon wedges, for serving

The bright green sauce—reminiscent of cold hard cash—is what spawned its creator to name this oyster dish after the wealthy Rockefeller family. Legend has it that the original version of these baked bivalves got its green from a different ingredient (perhaps parsley or capers), but spinach works swimmingly.

———————————

Preheat the oven to 350° F. On a baking sheet, parcook the bacon for 8 to 10 minutes, or until cooked but still tender. (This will allow the bacon a chance to crisp up in the next step.) Remove from the oven and cool. Chop the parcooked bacon into chunky bits.

Drain off 1 tablespoon of bacon grease and transfer to a large skillet. Heat over medium-high heat. Add the chopped bacon and garlic, and stir together. Then add the spinach and cook down, about 5 minutes. Add the heavy cream, Parmesan, cream cheese, salt, and pepper. Mix until thick and creamy. Then cool.

Meanwhile, place the oysters on a baking sheet. Add a couple tablespoons of the spinach mix on top of each fresh oyster. Bake in the oven for 12 minutes, or until the cheese is bubbling. Remove, sprinkle with green onions, and serve immediately with a sprig of parsley and a wedge of lemon.

TIP! Need help on how to shuck oysters? See the how-to tips on pages 47 and 142.

STEAMED MUSSELS OR CLAMS

Served in the shells that house them, mussels and clams can be cooked up using the same method. Just be sure to have the **Clam Nectar** prepped and ready to pour, as this dish comes together quickly.

_____

In a steamer pot over medium-high heat, fill the bottom with water (no salt needed) and bring to a boil. Steam the mussels or clams until their shells open, about 3 to 4 minutes. Any longer and they will get chewy. Discard any shells that do not open in the cooking process.

Transfer the bivalves into a large bowl. Pour the nectar over the top of the clams/mussels, sprinkle with the green onions, and serve.

Makes 4 servings

2 pounds mussels or clams
1¼ cups **Clam Nectar** (page 154)
    or alternate clam nectar
Chopped green onions, for garnish

Special equipment:

Steamer pot

All About Pacific Northwest Clams, Oysters, and Mussels

Clams, oysters, and mussels are known as bivalves, the name deriving from the two hinged shells (or valves) that open and close on either side of their bodies. Clams, oysters, and mussels live in intertidal zones along coastlines. Many seafood counters and restaurants in the Puget Sound area, including the Crab Pot Restaurant, purchase from farms such as Penn Cove Shellfish on Whidbey Island, north of Seattle.

Clams: Clams have little feet that extend out of their shells to help them burrow into sandy, muddy, or gravelly substrates. These bivalves feed on plankton and detritus by filtering small bits of this food from the water around them, cleaning the water and recycling its nutrients in the process. They also aerate sediments, contributing to overall marine health.

Wild clams can generally be harvested year-round, subject to local restrictions and water quality reports, but they are most readily accessible during the spring and early summer months. Farmed clams are often available year-round, although their shelf lives may be shorter if harvested during spawning season.

The Manila clams (*Venerupis philippinarum*), Native littleneck clams (*Leukoma staminea*), and butter clams (*Saxidomus giganteus*) all have a classic clam-like appearance with smooth, symmetrical shells. They are often light brown, tan, or even white on the outside, while the interior of their shells can be purple or other colors. The Manila, which originally came to North America in the 1940s as a stowaway with young oyster seeds, is the most popular.

Pacific razor clams (*Siliqua patula*) are larger than the Manila and elongated. The geoduck (*Panopea abrupta*), pronounced "gooey duck," is a bizarre species that looks a bit like a clam shell with a huge extended finger emerging from within—up to ten inches in length. The state of Washington produces the most farmed geo-ducks worldwide.

Oysters: These shellfish have rough, irregularly shaped brown, gray, or white shells and grow up to twelve inches long. They often live in large oyster reefs, known as natural sets, and attach themselves to shoreline rocks and to each other. Like other mollusks, they filter feed and thereby clean the waters where they live, and their flavors depend largely on where they are raised. Five oysters commonly found in the Pacific Northwest include the popular Pacific (*Crassostrea gigas*), which originated in Japan; the tiny Olympia, which encompasses two distinct species (*Ostrea conchaphila* and *Ostrea lurida*) and is native to the region; the sweet and creamy Kumamoto (*Crassostrea sikamea*), also originating in Asia; the Eastern (*Crassostrea virginica*), which is native to the northwestern Atlantic; and the European flats (*Ostrea edulis*), which comes from the northeastern Atlantic region. As with other shellfish, they are best if harvested when they aren't spawning, generally during the colder months.

Mussels: The two predominant mussels of the Pacific Northwest are the Mediterranean (*Mytilus galloprovincialis*), which, as the name implies, comes originally from the Mediterranean region, and the Pacific blue, also known as the Penn Cove mussel (*Mytilus trossulus*). Both are oblong, sport an iridescent blue-black shell, and live in dense colonies with their thin, fibrous beards helping them cling to rocks or each other. Although both naturally grow in the wild around Puget Sound, most mussels that show up at restaurants or at the seafood counter are farmed using suspension systems in shallow coastal waters. The Penn Cove spawns in the spring, and the Mediterranean spawns in the early winter. Both take about a year to be ready to harvest.

BREADED CALAMARI

Makes 4 servings

Oil, for frying
1 cup **Beer Batter** (page 163)
1 cup panko
4 (6-ounce) calamari steaks
Parsley sprigs, for serving
Lemon wedges, for serving

Special equipment:

Deep fryer

Calamari is a type of squid—but there are no visible arms and tentacles here. Instead, you'll use square steak calamari, sliced thin to bread and deep-fry this beer-battered delight.

———————————

Set up your deep fryer with oil and set it to 350° F.

Prepare two medium-sized dipping bowls by measuring out the beer batter into one bowl and the panko into the other. Set both aside.

Cut each steak into seven or so long thin strips. Rinse all. Then dip each piece first into the bowl of beer batter, followed by a dip into the panko bowl, making sure to coat each piece thoroughly and evenly with each dipping. As you work, place each breaded slice aside onto a wooden board or baking sheet with some room in between so the strips won't stick together.

Deep-fry the squid until golden brown, about 5 minutes. Remove from the fryer and set onto a paper towel–lined plate to soak up the excess oil.

Serve hot with a dipping sauce of your choice alongside parsley sprigs and lemon wedges.

> NOTE: *If you do not own a deep fryer, you can fill up a deep pot or Dutch oven with enough oil to submerge the calamari steaks. Fry them in 350° F oil.*

All About Pacific Northwest Squid

Many are surprised to learn that squid is another type of shellfish, although its shell, known as a pen or cuttlebone, is inside the body. It is classified as a cephalopod, which literally means "head foot," referring to the proximity between the head and the tentacles, or arms. Most squid (*Doryteuthis (Loligo) opalescens*) consumed in the Pacific Northwest come from California and are also known as the California market squid. They have a head, two eyes, two tentacles, and eight arms all extending from the same end of its whitish-purplish, iridescent body. They grow to about twelve inches in length and only live for six to nine months, first at depths up to 2,600 feet but then moving into shallow waters, in large schools, when it is time to spawn.

Fishermen seek out squid at night, shining bright lights into the water to attract the schools. They then gather up the squid by casting out purse seines—large nets with rings along the bottom of the net and steel lines or ropes threaded through the rings that can be drawn shut when the school of squid swims into the targeted area. If the squid somehow aren't caught during the spawning process, they die afterward.

COCONUT PRAWNS

Makes 12 prawns

Oil, for frying
12 (16/20) shrimp, peeled and
    deveined
1½ cups shredded coconut
⅓ cup flour
1½ cups panko, divided
1½ cups **Beer Batter** (page 163)
Sweet chili sauce, for dipping
Parsley sprigs, for serving
Lemon wedges, for serving

Special equipment:

Deep fryer

Blending panko with coconut renders a sweet and crunchy flavor for the tender meat inside. In this case, that is 16/20 shrimp. Shrimp size is measured by count and so its "number" refers to how many shrimp you'll get in one pound. These jumbo-sized crustaceans are served with sweet chili sauce—the cherry on top of this popular seafood starter.

Set up your deep fryer with oil and set it to 350° F.

Rinse the shrimp under cool running water and set aside.

In a medium bowl, mix the coconut with the flour and ¼ cup of the panko (this is so the coconut will stick to the shrimp). Prepare two other medium dipping bowls by measuring out the beer batter into one bowl and the remaining panko into the other.

Dip each shrimp first into the bowl of beer batter, then in the panko, followed by the coconut mixture, making sure to coat each shrimp thoroughly and evenly with each dipping. As you work, place each shrimp aside onto a wooden board or baking sheet with some room in between so the shrimp won't stick together.

Deep-fry until golden brown, about 5 minutes. Remove from the fryer and set onto a paper towel–lined plate to soak up the excess oil.

Serve hot with sweet chili sauce alongside parsley sprigs and lemon wedges.

NOTE: *If you do not own a deep fryer, you can fill up a deep pot or Dutch oven with enough oil to submerge the prawns. Fry them in 350° F oil.*

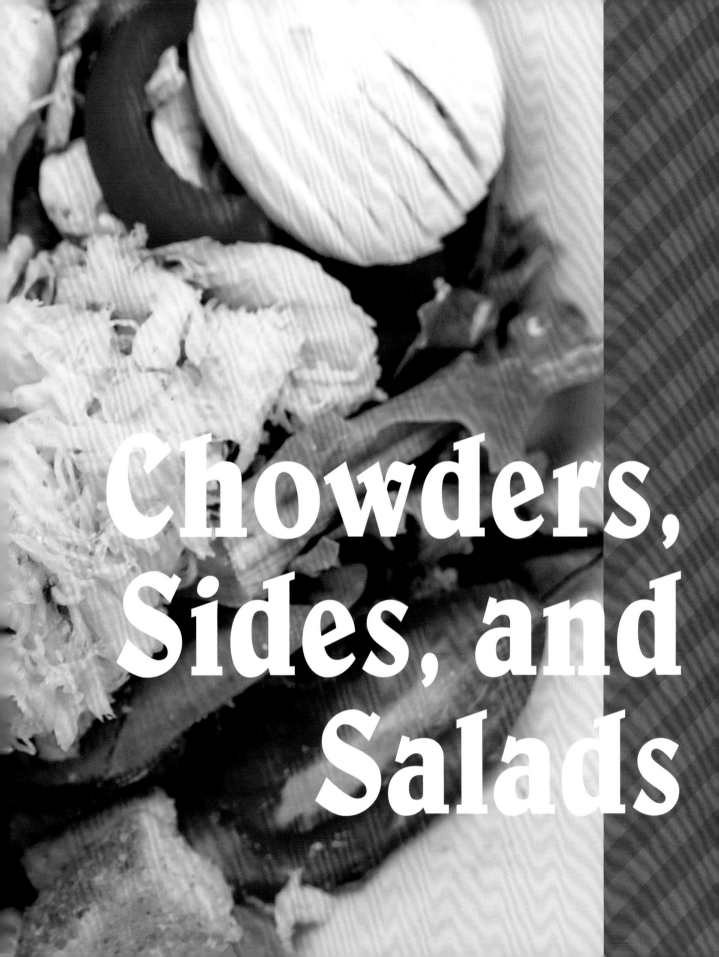

Chowders, Sides, and Salads

CLAM CHOWDER

Makes 12 servings

2 cups unsalted butter

1¾ cups all-purpose flour

2 tablespoons vegetable oil

6 cups diced yellow onion (about 3 medium)

3 cups chopped celery (about 6 ribs)

2 teaspoons minced garlic

1½ teaspoons dried thyme

1½ teaspoons dried basil

1½ teaspoons dried oregano

1½ teaspoons ground black pepper

½ gallon (8 cups) whole milk

2 (8-ounce) jars clam juice

1 cup clam base

1 (51-ounce) can or 8 (6.5-ounce) cans chopped sea or ocean clams

2½ pounds potatoes, a mix of red and russet (about 2 large of each), peeled and diced small

Red, white, or pink? Who knew the world of chowder mirrors the world of wine? Here is the Crab Pot's white clam chowder, which omits the tomato ingredients of its red counterpart, Manhattan, as well as lobster or salmon, which results in a pink version, as seen in **Salmon Chowder** (page 89). Clam base is the thick bouillon that gives the broth its flavor. It's salty, so don't add salt while sweating the vegetables and make sure to use unsalted butter. If clam base isn't available at your local market, substitute with chicken or beef bouillon base.

NOTE: *This chowder makes enough for a crowd, so be sure to use a large stockpot, at least 8 quarts.*

To make the roux, in a large pot over low heat, add the butter and cook until melted. Add the flour, stirring until combined, and cook, stirring often, until the mixture is golden brown, about 10 minutes. Set aside.

In a separate large stockpot over high heat, heat the oil. Add the onion, celery, and garlic. Cook, stirring often, until the onion is translucent, about 5 minutes. Add the thyme, basil, oregano, and pepper. Cook the vegetables on medium heat for another few minutes, until they get a little bit of color. Add the milk, clam juice, and clam base, stir to combine, and bring to a boil.

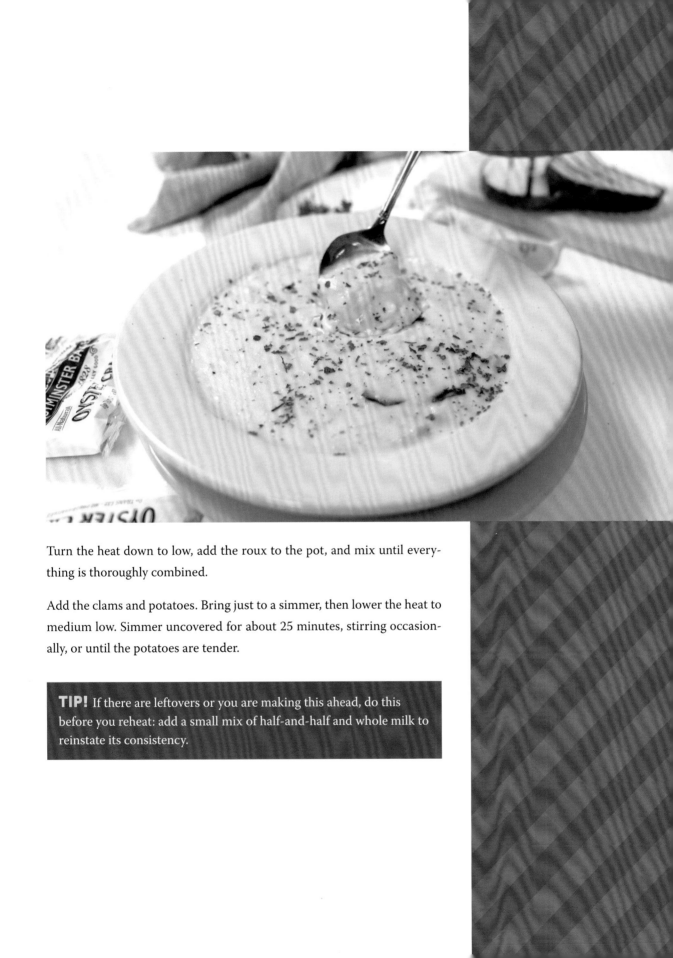

Turn the heat down to low, add the roux to the pot, and mix until everything is thoroughly combined.

Add the clams and potatoes. Bring just to a simmer, then lower the heat to medium low. Simmer uncovered for about 25 minutes, stirring occasionally, or until the potatoes are tender.

TIP! If there are leftovers or you are making this ahead, do this before you reheat: add a small mix of half-and-half and whole milk to reinstate its consistency.

SALMON CHOWDER

Salmon chowder is an incredibly wholesome alternative to creamy clam chowder. Tender, flaky salmon pieces and its marinara sauce—tinted and flavored broth are at the heart of this pinkish chowder. Take the color theme one step further by pairing this hearty chowder with some rosé. If you prefer a smaller amount, this recipe is easily scaled down.

Makes 12 servings

4 (3-ounce) andouille sausages, diced small

2 tablespoons butter or oil

4 cups chopped yellow onion (about 2 medium)

1½ cups chopped celery (about 4 ribs)

1 tablespoon minced garlic

12 cups water

1 (8-ounce) jar chicken base

1 (8-ounce) jar clam base

1 (12-ounce) bag whole kernel corn, frozen

2 red bell peppers, finely chopped

1 green bell pepper, finely chopped

¼ cup lemon juice (from 1 lemon)

2 pounds red potatoes (about 8 medium), diced

1½ cups marinara sauce

Kosher salt

Freshly ground black pepper

20 ounces smoked salmon

NOTE: If you're using a chicken bouillon cube instead of thick chicken base, do not dissolve it in additional water. Just let it dissolve in the mixture.

In a frying pan over medium-high heat, brown the sausage, about 3 minutes. Set aside.

In a stockpot over medium-high heat, heat the butter or oil. Add the onion, celery, and garlic, and sauté until the onions are sweaty, about 5 minutes. Add the cooked sausage and stir together. Add the water, chicken base, clam base, corn, peppers, and lemon juice. Stir to combine. Then add the potatoes and marinara and bring to a boil, about 20 minutes. Salt and pepper to taste. When ready to serve, portion out the salmon in each bowl, sprinkling it on top.

PACIFIC NORTHWEST SEAFOOD LOUIE SALAD

Why make this salad? It's simple *and* impressive. It's delicious *and* healthy. It's a masterpiece of arrangement *and* makes a full meal. Plus, if you happen to have leftover salmon in the fridge, you won't heat up the house cooking it on a hot summer day.

Makes 4 large salads

8 ounces salmon
6 cups mixed spring greens
8 ounces cooked crabmeat
8 ounces cooked bay shrimp
1 small tomato, sliced into wedges
⅓ cup sliced mushrooms
½ cucumber, sliced into rounds
¼ cup croutons
½ red bell pepper, sliced in rounds
4 hard-boiled eggs
Salad dressing of choice
Cabbage wedge, for serving
    (optional)

In a small frying pan, cook the salmon using your preferred method.

Onto each bowl/plate, lay a foundation of the mixed greens. Working around the plate in a circle, scoop a portion of salmon, crab, and shrimp, followed by the tomatoes, mushrooms, cucumbers, and croutons. Add a ring of bell pepper in the center of the circle, and top with a sliced hard-boiled egg.

Offer your fellow diners the dressing of their choice. Serve it in a cabbage triangle, and let them toss together their Louie at the table.

VARIATION: *If the fish part of this Louie is too much variety for your taste buds, use any combination of 1½ pounds of prepared seafood for an equally good Louie.*

WATERMELON SALAD WITH SUMMER SEASONAL DRESSING

Makes 4 servings

For the dressing:

¾ cup extra-virgin olive oil
½ cup lemon juice (from 2 lemons)
2¼ teaspoons Crab Pot Seaspice
  or alternate seafood seasoning
1½ teaspoons chopped fresh basil
1½ teaspoons chopped fresh mint
¼ teaspoon salt
¼ teaspoon cayenne pepper

For the salad:

3 cups cubed watermelon
2¼ cups cubed cucumber (about 2
  cucumbers)
⅓ cup feta cheese sprinkles
1 tablespoon chopped fresh basil

When the clouds part in the Pacific Northwest, fresh fruit makes its appearance as the Crab Pot's seasonal salad offering. Watermelon is at the center of this particular summer salad topped with a zesty dressing made Mexican-style with cayenne pepper for some summertime heat.

In a large bowl, whisk together the oil, lemon juice, Seaspice, basil, mint, salt, and pepper until blended. Add the watermelon and cucumber, and stir to coat. Sprinkle the feta and basil on top of the salad, and serve.

RICE PILAF

The Crab Pot chefs make pilaf with long-grain rice, which looks like brown rice. But any rice you have on hand will work—though wild rice is the healthiest option. No matter what you choose, do note that this fluffy, nutty pilaf is prepared in the oven and makes a delicious—and absorbent—side dish to soak up all the juices left over from any dish.

Makes about 3 cups

⅛ cup chicken base (from a jar)
2 cups water
1 teaspoon minced garlic
1 bay leaf
Pinch of salt
Pinch of ground black pepper
1 cup uncooked rice
1 cup sliced mushrooms
1 tablespoon oil

Preheat the oven to 275° F.

In a large bowl, dissolve the chicken base in the water. Mix in the garlic, bay leaf, salt, and pepper. Transfer to a deep baking dish. Add the uncooked rice, and stir together. Cover the dish with plastic wrap and foil, and bake for 45 minutes.

At about 15 minutes before the rice is done, sauté the mushrooms in a frying pan with the oil. Cool and set aside.

When the rice is done, fluffy with all the water absorbed, remove it from the oven, pull out the bay leaf, and stir in the mushrooms. Serve as a side note to any dish.

TIP! The plastic wrap shouldn't melt in the oven. The Crab Pot chefs use it to keep the condensation that forms on the foil in the steaming process from adding moisture into the rice.

The *Gail Force*

As part of his vision for Miners Landing and the Crab Pot Restaurant, Hal purchased a forty-six-foot commercial fishing boat from a multi-generational crab-fishing family located on the southern coast of Washington. Built in Mount Vernon, Washington, the *Gail Force* was specifically designed to fish for Dungeness crab in and around the shallow waters of Willapa Bay, a niche fishery in an intertidal zone that is heavily populated with crabs and other sea life. By vertically integrating this component of the restaurant's supply chain, the costs associated with one of the most expensive ingredients on the menu can be kept in check. In addition, the Griffith family can be assured that sustainable practices are used, the restaurant's carbon footprint is minimized, and local fishermen supplying the crabs are directly supported. "It's the same sort of concept as farm-to-table restaurants," Kyle says.

And in the same way that farmers work long, hard days to grow the corn and potatoes in the Seafeast, the crew of the *Gail Force* puts in fourteen to sixteen hours a day during the crabbing season. The captain, who has decades of maritime experience, and the crew often wind up doing much of their work in the cold, windy dark beneath sodium or LED lights, given that the peak of the season (normally December and January) coincides with the shortest days, and most inclement weather, of the year, which means the crew needs to start early—around 4:00 a.m.—to get to all their crab pots each day. The boat is licensed to have five hundred crab pots in the water at a time, and the pots can fill up daily. That means that once a day they need to be hoisted onto the boat, emptied, re-baited with squid and razor clams, and re-set into the water. Depending on the size of the crabs caught, each pot could yield fifty mature males, and on a good day early in the season, it's conceivable the *Gail Force* might bring in twenty-five thousand crabs in a single day.

It's a demanding job, and crab fishing isn't for the faint of heart. As featured on the Discovery Channel's show *Deadliest Catch*, it is considered one of the most dangerous jobs in the world. Angry crabs can break your fingers with their claws, and you can hurt yourself managing the multi-ton crab pots, even with hydraulic equipment. Or you can be knocked off the boat into the water. Turbulent weather, rogue waves, and unstable working conditions on roiling seas can turn a normal day on the job into a deadly one. Work on the *Gail Force* is treacherous, brutal, and demanding, with spits and other land features that are difficult to navigate, a rapid pace of handling five hundred pots each day, and a long season (often running from December through August). Because the fishermen have so little time at home, it's a profession that can put a lot of strain on the family. And once the season ends, there are only a few months to perform all the required maintenance tasks on the boat and the pots before the next season starts. It's a lifestyle that requires sacrifice and commitment, but one that can be lucrative in good years, depending on fishing and market conditions.

Entrées

SEAFOOD COMBO SKEWER

Makes 8 skewers

16 button mushrooms
1 pound halibut fillet, cut into
    chunks
1 pound steelhead salmon fillet,
    cut into chunks
1 medium-sized red onion, diced
    large
1 medium-sized red bell pepper,
    diced large
1 medium-sized green bell pepper,
    diced large
Oil, for frying
Dried parsley, for garnish
Kosher salt
Freshly ground black pepper

Special equipment:

Bamboo skewers

Capped with button mushrooms, the Crab Pot's seafood skewers are a *misto* of fish and veggies. Follow this recipe to the T for a balance of both aesthetic and palate-pleasing delight. Or trade out ingredients, making a custom combo that includes shrimp or any sturdy fish or vegetable easily skewered and seared.

———————————

On a skewer, pierce one mushroom cap side first to act as an anchor. Then add a chunk of each ingredient, repeating once or until you are near the end of the skewer, then cap it off with a second mushroom, cap side out. Repeat with the remaining skewers.

In a frying pan over medium-high heat, add enough oil to coat the pan. Grill the skewers on both sides until the fish is firm and the veggies are soft, about 6 to 8 minutes. Remove from the pan, sprinkle with dried parsley, and season to taste with salt and pepper. Serve at once.

All About Pacific Northwest Halibut

The Pacific halibut (*Hippoglossus stenolepis*) is the largest flatfish in the ocean. It is diamond shaped and a mottled brown or gray color, so it blends in with the colors of the seafloor. Able to grow up to six hundred pounds and eight feet long, the Pacific halibut can live up to twenty-five years or more.

The young halibut, hatched during winter months, has a bizarre beginning to its life. When first hatched from its egg, the round fish has eyes situated on each side of its head, like most fish, and it floats through the water. But by the time it's about six months old and has made a home on the ocean floor, it has gone through an amazing transformation: it has flattened out, and its eyes have shifted position so that both wind up on just one side of the head—the upper side, so the fish can watch the ocean above as it moves about near the seafloor. At this point, it swims sideways.

The Pacific halibut preys aggressively on a variety of shellfish and other finfish, and when young it can be hunted and caught by large marine mammals and sharks. Once it is large and mature, it is rarely preyed upon by other animals.

The Native peoples of the region used wooden hooks attached to rocks, with octopus used as bait, to catch halibut. Many traditional fishing practices like this are still used by Native people today. Commercial fishermen now catch it with long lines that are draped along the seafloor with intermittently spaced hooks. As each fish is snagged, it's brought up to the boat to be killed and set on ice. Most are harvested in Alaska, although they can also be found off the coasts of Oregon, Washington, and British Columbia. Fishing season for Pacific halibut is generally March through November, and they are generally caught when they are substantially smaller than what they might become. Typically, they are harvested when they are thirty pounds or so.

With its slightly sweet and mild flavor, halibut is a favorite on many dinner plates.

CRAB–STUFFED KING SALMON

Makes 4 servings

4 (6-ounce) fillets of king salmon

1¾ cups **Crab Cake** mix (page 64)

4 teaspoons **Grilling Butter** (page 162), for garnish

Dried parsley, for garnish

Kosher salt

1 recipe **Rice Pilaf** (page 95)

Vegetables of your choice, sliced (optional)

Special equipment:

4 individual ceramic baking dishes (optional)

You can't really go wrong with a dish that calls for seafood stuffed with more seafood, especially when that stuffing is a crowd-pleasing crab cake mix. And it only *looks* complicated. The Crab Pot chefs prefer king salmon from the Columbia River or from their neighbors in Alaska. Whatever salmon you choose, just look for thick cuts for the best possible results.

Preheat the oven to 350° F.

Butterfly the fillet lengthwise (slicing almost in half, but leaving wings). Line the inside of the fillets with the crab mix stuffing in a thin, even layer. Fold the wing back over to fully cover the stuffing. Repeat for each fillet, and place onto a baking sheet or into individual dishes. Bake for 15 minutes or until the fish flakes easily with a fork.

Remove from the oven and ladle the butter over the fillets. Sprinkle with dried parsley and season to taste with salt. Serve with a scoop of rice pilaf and sliced vegetables of your choice.

TIP! This fish fits easily into a medium-sized oval ceramic dish, which can go straight from the oven to the table.

All About Pacific Northwest Salmon

When asked what they first think about when hearing the term "Pacific Northwest cuisine," most people will immediately come up with *salmon*. And for good reason: Salmon came to the region ten to fifteen million years ago, long before people did and even before the mountains were formed. They were here during the last ice age and survived by migrating around the frozen rivers.

To the Native peoples of the Pacific Northwest, the salmon are extremely important. In one Indigenous folk story, the Creator asked the animals what they might do to help humans who, without their help, wouldn't know how to survive. Salmon offered its body as sustenance, with two conditions: first, Salmon would be allowed to return to its birthplace and, second, the humans would be willing to speak up for Salmon whenever Salmon wasn't able to speak on its own behalf. If the fish wasn't properly treated, it would refuse to return to the river to make itself available for future food.

The story, of course, refers to the salmon's anadromous life cycle. The salmon is born inland, in fresh water, after two months of incubation, and then it spends the next few months in rivers trying to avoid being eaten. When the time is right, it begins its long journey to the ocean, where it will spend most of the rest of its life, which can mean hundreds of miles of swimming. Assuming it hasn't been caught by predators or otherwise eliminated by disease or starvation, the fish will one day instinctively return to its river of origin bulked up on food in preparation for the long journey. Once there, it stops feeding and swims for its life, literally—fighting its way for miles upstream, over rocks and rapids and alongside other salmon, until it reaches its birthplace. There, the females deposit their eggs. The males fertilize them. And then they die.

Indigenous people have gone to great lengths to honor the

salmon, including holding first-salmon ceremonies to honor the first fish caught in each season. In fact, as described in David M. Buerge's book *Chief Seattle and the Town That Took His Name: The Change of Worlds for the Native People and Settlers on Puget Sound*, the Duwamish people and an elderly Chief Seattle were celebrating the first salmon run of the season one spring when a few Americans came upon them. Buerge writes that Chief Seattle explained the festivities to the visitors. "As the salmon are our chief food, we always rejoice to see them coming early and in abundance, for that ensures us a plentiful quantity of food for the coming winter. This is the reason our hearts are glad today." In such ceremonies, the fish would be sprinkled with sacred material, such as eagle down, and great speeches would be made as morsels of the cooked fish were distributed to each person.

Five species of salmon are found in the Pacific Northwest, British Columbia, and Alaska. (The steelhead, which many believe to be a type of salmon, is actually a trout. It behaves, tastes, and looks much like salmon, but it survives the spawning process.) The flavors and fat content of each species, and within each species, vary depending on where the fish were hatched and what foods they ate in their youth. The Columbia River in Washington State has long been considered a premier salmon river, and some estimates suggest that, just a couple of hundred years ago—prior to the arrival of the Europeans—this river's annual salmon runs included tens of millions of fish. Other popular rivers for salmon and steelhead—and likewise for anglers—in the region include the Willamette, Rogue, and Umpqua Rivers in Oregon and the Cowlitz, Hoh, Skagit, and Snake Rivers in Washington. The Fraser River in British Columbia was once a hub for salmon and their predators, although recent years have seen a decline in the salmon population there. Alaska's Copper River is home to king, sockeye, and coho salmon and is credited with the quality of those fish because of the especially long,

arduous run the salmon need to make in order to spawn and the quantity of healthy fat packed on before the journey.

Salmon is considered a keystone species, serving as an important component of the entire Pacific Northwest ecosystem. It's a nutrient-dense food source for human beings, grizzly bears, orcas, seals, and other mammals as well as for predatory birds. It also keeps the population of its own prey, including crustaceans and smaller fish, in check. And it enriches the entire ecosystem by processing nutrients throughout its journeys from inland freshwater rivers to the ocean and back again.

Of the five species, the Chinook, also known as the king (*Oncorhynchus tshawytscha*), is the largest, often weighing in at twenty-five pounds or more. It has the highest fat content and, therefore, the most exquisite flavor—and most expensive price tag.

The sockeye, also known as red salmon (*Oncorhynchus nerka*), is a medium-sized fish at six to nine pounds. The coho, also known as the silver salmon (*Oncorhynchus kisutch*), is similar in size to the sockeye at six to twelve pounds. The pink (*Oncorhynchus gorbuscha*) is the smallest at just three to twelve pounds and tends to be more abundant than some of the other varieties. As it is also much leaner, it is usually sold canned or smoked. And finally, the chum, also known as dog salmon (*Oncorhynchus keta*), ranges from six to seventeen pounds. The last to spawn each year, it also tends to be a lean fish and more affordable than the other species.

The steelhead (*Oncorhynchus mykiss*) is Washington's state fish.

It can grow up to forty pounds and prefers smaller, fast-moving rivers. Because of its status as a threatened species, most steelhead found in restaurants and fish counters have been farm raised.

Salmon was originally caught by the Coast Salish and other regional Indigenous tribes from canoes, using spears or nets. Weirs made from stone, brush, or wood were also erected across rivers, and, as the fish swam through small openings, the men caught them in baskets or nets. Occasionally, fires and torches were set up along riverbanks to attract the fish, which were then caught with nets or spears.

With industrialization came new methods for harvesting salmon, and by the early 1900s the Alaskan salmon fisheries were the largest in the world. Nowadays, salmon are harvested commercially using one of three methods: purse seining, which involves a net stretched between a small boat and a larger boat that then encircles the school of fish; trolling, which involves using several fishing lines from a boat and catching the fish individually; and gill nets, which trap fish as they swim by and are so named because the fish's gills get caught up in the net when they try to escape.

Industrialization also brought new methods for preserving salmon. At first, salmon were initially exported from the region in barrels, but the fish often rotted before arriving at their destinations. Then along came canneries, with the first salmon cannery being founded on the Columbia River soon after the Washington Territory was established in 1853. By the mid-1880s, there were at least fifty canneries in the Columbia River Basin alone, which extends across much of what is now Washington State, and by the turn of the century Whatcom County had eleven of its own. Salmon became an affordable staple of many diets, and thousands of local fishermen earned their livings by supplying fish to the canneries. Competition among them was fierce, and the drive toward prosperity fueled an economic boom in the industry. By 1900, one million cases of canned salmon were shipped annually from Washington's canneries.

CIOPPINO

Pronounced *chuh-PEE-no*, this rustic soup is a blend of seafood goodness also known as fisherman's stew—so called for the mariners who first enjoyed what was a medley of leftovers and bread. The Crab Pot's is neatly contained in a bread bowl ready to eat in its entirety.

For the sauce, in a stockpot over medium-high heat, heat the oil. Add the onion, celery, bell pepper, and carrot, and sauté until tiny bits of brown start to show. Add the tomatoes, clam juice, garlic, clam base, black pepper, oregano, basil, and cayenne pepper. Bring it to a slow rolling boil, about 5 minutes.

To make the stew, add the nectar, crab, clams, mussels, and salmon to the sauce. Bring to a boil. Then reduce the heat and let simmer until the clams and mussels open, about 4 minutes.

Meanwhile, slice the top off each boule and remove the soft center to create the bread bowls. When the stew is ready, ladle it into the boule bowls, dispersing evenly.

TIP! Use the leftover bread to assist in making a batch of the **Crab Pot Bread Pudding** (page 169) or breadcrumbs for **World-Famous Crab Pot Mac & Cheese** (page 128).

Makes 4 servings

For the sauce:

⅛ cup olive oil
¼ cup diced yellow onion
¼ cup diced celery
¼ cup diced green bell pepper
⅛ cup shredded carrot
1 (28-ounce) can crushed tomatoes
¾ cup clam juice
1 tablespoon chopped fresh garlic
1½ teaspoons clam base
¼ teaspoon ground black pepper
Pinch of dried oregano
Pinch of dried basil
Pinch of cayenne pepper

For the stew:

1 recipe **Clam Nectar** (page 154) or 4 cups alternate clam nectar
2 pounds Dungeness crab sections
24 clams (about 1 pound), scrubbed and rinsed
24 mussels (about 1 pound), scrubbed and rinsed
8 ounces smoked salmon
4 (8-ounce) sourdough boules

WORLD-FAMOUS CRAB POT BURGER

Makes 4 servings

1½ pounds ground beef

2 teaspoons seasoning salt

8 strips bacon

4 large hamburger buns

1 cup **Honey Mustard Dressing**
  (page 161), divided

4 slices lettuce

4 slices tomato

4 slices yellow onion

4 slices American cheese

Cabbage wedge, for serving
  (optional)

4 dill pickles, for serving (optional)

French fries (optional)

Not much on the Crab Pot menu is seafood-free, but rest assured that this burger isn't there just for the one person at the table who doesn't like fish. In fact, this colossal bacon cheeseburger is world famous and just as celebrated as any of the more to-theme offerings. It's a lesson in how a lot of singular items come together to make something special. Better together, personified.

In a medium bowl, add the ground beef and seasoning salt, and mix together by hand. Form into four patties and set aside.

In a frying pan over medium-high heat, cook the bacon until brown, turning once. Remove the bacon from the pan and drain off the excess oil, but leave enough so the bottom of the pan is coated. Cook the patties to your desired doneness (the Crab Pot chefs suggest medium rare), turning once.

Meanwhile, toast the buns and slather with some of the dressing. When the patties are ready, build your colossal burger like this: bottom bun, lettuce, tomato, onion, meat patty, cheese, bacon, top bun. Spoon the remaining dressing into a cabbage triangle.

Serve with a pickle and some french fries.

SHRIMP TACOS

Makes 8 tacos

24 (16/20) shrimp, peeled and deveined

2 tablespoons seasoning salt

2 tablespoons margarine

8 (6-inch) table-style flour or corn tortillas

1 cup **Tomato Herb Aioli** (page 155)

1 cup mixed red/green cabbage

1 recipe **Pico de Gallo** (page 157) or 1 cup alternate pico de gallo

1 cup salsa

Cabbage wedge, for serving (optional)

Tortilla chips (optional)

As in many of the Crab Pot dishes, the foundational element in these tacos is the spice. Made with blackened 16/20 jumbo shrimp (16/20 refers to how many pieces are in a pound) grilled up with your choice of seasoning salt, this taco duet with or without a side of chips is a fulfilling meal any day of the week.

In a medium bowl, add the shrimp, seasoning salt, and margarine, and mix together by hand.

In a frying pan over medium-high heat, grill the shrimp until cooked and charred, about 2 minutes per side. Set aside. Then, in the same pan, heat each tortilla, turning once.

Prepare each taco in this order: tortilla, aioli, three pieces of shrimp, cabbage, and pico de gallo. Spoon the salsa into a cabbage triangle. Serve up two tacos per plate alongside a handful of tortilla chips.

All About Pacific Northwest Shrimp

Most shellfish live near shorelines, and they all have soft bodies, some of which are protected by hard outer shells. The spot prawn (*Pandalus platyceros*), also known as the spot shrimp, is named for the white spots on its body and lives up and down the West Coast from Southern California to Alaska's Aleutian Islands. Although a bottom feeder preferring muddy seafloors and rocky outcroppings where it can forage for worms, sponges, algae, and other shellfish, the spot prawn migrates seasonally between deeper and shallow waters. It grows to about nine inches in length, often switches its gender from male to female during its lifetime, and serves as prey for large fish such as halibut, cod, and salmon.

Indigenous women often dug for spot prawns using long sticks. Nowadays, commercial fishermen catch spot prawns with traps. Fisheries are highly regulated, with only a few days—or sometimes hours—open each year to spot prawn harvesting around Puget Sound, where the daily catch can be limited to no more than eighty per day. Out in the Pacific Ocean, where shrimp grounds are at least thirty miles from shore—and inaccessible to most sport fishing boats—there are fewer restrictions, and the shrimp are more readily available with larger daily maximums of up to two hundred prawns.

Pink shrimp (*Pandalus jordani)*, also known as bay shrimp, are also commonly harvested, and served, in the Pacific Northwest. Its season runs from mid-spring to mid-fall, extending longer in northern waters. The wild pink shrimp is often caught by trawling, a method considered unacceptable for many other types of seafood due to the likelihood of inadvertently catching other marine animals. However, modern shrimp nets incorporate devices to minimize unintended bycatch and are stretched out in midwater, rather than on the ocean floor, reducing the likelihood of snagging unwanted fish or other animals.

SALMON TACOS

For some, a taco is the perfect meal: a healthy balance of all the food groups presented in an edible container. Here's your chance to improve upon perfection: turn up the heat on Taco Tuesday with a simple **Chipotle Aioli** and **Pico de Gallo**.

———————————

In a frying pan over medium-high heat, grill the salmon until it starts to brown, turning once, about 3 or 4 minutes. Set aside. Then, in the same pan, heat each tortilla, turning once.

Prepare each taco in this order: tortilla, aioli, two pieces of salmon, cabbage, and pico de gallo. Spoon the salsa into a cabbage triangle. Serve to each hungry diner two tacos alongside a handful of tortilla chips.

Makes 8 tacos

1 pound salmon, cut into 16 strips from a whole fillet
8 (6-inch) table-style flour or corn tortillas
1 recipe **Chipotle Aioli** (page 156) or 1 cup alternate aioli
1 cup mixed red/green cabbage
1 recipe **Pico de Gallo** (page 157) or 1 cup alternate pico de gallo
1 cup salsa
Cabbage wedge, for serving (optional)
Tortilla chips (optional)

VARIATION: Since tacos are infinitely customizable, here's a thought: use wahoo. It's a white fish that's in the spectrum between a lingcod and a tuna. Substitute it for the salmon and **Tartar Sauce** *(page 150) for the aioli—and be prepared to welcome this pairing into your regular rotation.*

WORLD-FAMOUS CRAB POT MAC & CHEESE

Makes 4 servings

For the breadcrumbs:

1 torpedo roll (or sourdough boule leftovers)
¼ cup shredded Parmesan cheese
1 tablespoon dried parsley

For the pasta:

1 (16-ounce) package radiatori pasta
6 tablespoons butter
2 tablespoons fresh minced garlic
12 ounces red king crab
Kosher salt
Freshly ground black pepper
1⅛ cups heavy cream
¾ cup grated white and yellow blend of cheddar cheese
¾ cup shredded Parmesan cheese, plus more for garnish
Dried parsley, for garnish
Chopped green onions, for garnish

The *mac* is bite-sized radiatori pasta with lots of nooks and crannies to hold on to the three-cheese-y sauce and the chunks of red crab—a smaller, sweeter option to the richer, in taste and cost, Dungeness crabmeat. But this dish is easily interchangeable: mix and match with the same amounts of any crab or fish or scallops or shrimp or chicken or . . . No matter what you choose, this mac & cheese dish will be world famous at your house too.

———————————

Preheat the oven to 350° F.

To make the breadcrumbs, cut the roll into 1-inch cubes. On a baking sheet, spread out the cubes in one even layer and bake until slightly browned, about 3 minutes. When cooled, in a large bowl, break the cubes into crumbles. Add the Parmesan and dried parsley, and mix by hand until combined. Set aside.

Prepare the pasta to your desired doneness using the manufacturer's directions. Meanwhile, in a large pot over medium-high heat, add the butter and garlic and sauté for a few minutes. Add the crab and sauté a few more minutes. Season to taste with salt and pepper. Add the prepared pasta and cream, and bring to a boil. Add the cheddar and Parmesan. Stir together carefully until all of the ingredients are evenly distributed.

Transfer the mixture to a large baking dish, and bake for 2 minutes, until the cheese bubbles. Top with the prepared breadcrumbs and return the dish to the oven to cook for 40 seconds or until the breadcrumbs begin to get golden brown.

Sprinkle with the Parmesan, parsley, and green onions, and serve.

PIER 57 SMOKED SALMON FETTUCINE

Truth be told, Parmesan and pasta hold court for many a dish. Add to that foundation flaky bits of smoked salmon—all wrapped up in the long fettucine noodles swimming in the creamy rich sauce—and you'll soon be left with only the side of grilled sourdough ready to soak up every last bit.

_____

Prepare the pasta to your desired doneness per the manufacturer's instructions.

Meanwhile, in a frying pan over medium-high heat, heat the oil. Add the onion, capers, and garlic. Sauté until the onions are sweaty, about 3 minutes. Add the parsley and green onions, and stir. Then add the white wine and cook until reduced by two-thirds. Add the lemon juice and reduce. Add the cream and reduce. When the mixture begins to boil, add the prepared pasta, salmon, and ¾ cup of Parmesan-Romano. Sauté until the cheese is bubbly, about 3 minutes. Remove from the heat. Sprinkle with the remaining Parmesan-Romano, parsley, and green onions. Serve alongside grilled sourdough toast, if desired.

Makes 4 servings

1 (16-ounce) package fettucine
1 tablespoon oil
⅓ cup chopped red onion
3 ounces capers
2 tablespoons minced fresh garlic
3 sprigs flat-leaf parsley, chopped
3 green onions, chopped
¾ cup white cooking wine
3 tablespoons lemon juice (from 1 lemon)
3 cups heavy cream
12 ounces smoked salmon
1 cup shredded Parmesan-Romano (75-to-25) cheese mix, divided
Dried parsley, for garnish
Chopped green onions, for garnish
Grilled sourdough toast (optional)

Traditional Ways of Preparing, Cooking, and Serving Seafood

The combination of salty and fresh waters, expansive forests protecting clean rivers, and temperate climate of the Pacific Northwest have contributed to amazing seafood that offers a variety of unique flavors and textures. But seafood meat also tends to be more fragile than the meat of other animals and susceptible to over- or undercooking and spoilage. The Coast Salish and other Indigenous people of the region learned how to properly prepare the meats, and they did so without using eggs, dairy, or wheat to support the recipes. Instead, they used herbs, greens, roots, and other plants gathered locally, and natural fats from endemic sources. Three classic, traditional methods used by the Coast Salish were grilling, smoking, and steaming, with many types of seafood cooked on wooden racks made from branches set over the fire. And although historically they ate fresh food when possible, they developed methods to preserve their seafood through smoking and drying processes to store it for bleak winter months.

The Crab Pot Restaurant's smoked salmon fettuccine, and the Salmon Cooker Restaurant's alderwood-smoked fish entrées, recall the smoking methods used by the Coast Salish, with fish hanging over an alderwood fire. They also perfected the art of slow-cook steaming by first digging a hole in the dirt, then filling it with small branches, wood, and stones, and starting a fire within. When the fire had turned to coals, they lined the walls of the pit with fern leaves, which they also layered intermittently with the food being cooked. Finally, they punched a hole through the layers of fern, added water, and covered the pit. The food would steam for several hours.

In the early days, people also cooked their fish and shellfish by stone-boiling, a cooking method that involves heating stones over a large fire before placing them into a wooden box or basket with water, or other cooking liquids, and then adding the food to the pot. Hot stones were continually added to the food from the fire, throughout the cooking process, to keep the broth boiling until the meat was cooked and tender. Baking was traditionally accomplished using a rock oven, made from a pit dug into the soil and lined with wood and stones.

One other tradition that many Indigenous and other cultures adopted, as part of their cooking practices, was to use as much of the seafood as possible and to avoid food waste. For example, they used fish heads, tails, skin, and bones—the parts we normally wouldn't eat—to make a delicious stock.

When immigrants began to move into the area from China, Japan, the Philippines, Sweden, Russia, and other countries around the globe, they brought their own culinary preferences and traditions. By the early and middle years of the twentieth century, when the piers were bustling along the waterfront, Seattle's culinary repertoire had expanded. Some of the offerings were likely similar to what the Native peoples had eaten, including classically prepared Olympia oysters and Dungeness crab legs, while other recipes undoubtedly came from farther afield, like fish and chips or fish steamed with lemongrass.

Throughout the past two centuries, the region's culinary palate has continued to evolve as a blend of many cultures, which means that Pacific Northwest cuisine, by definition, is more than just salmon. It's a fusion of flavors even if salmon and crab are the guests of honor on the dinner table or at the Crab Pot Restaurant. Still, some of the traditions practiced by the Coast Salish underpin today's classic Pacific Northwest cuisine: finding the freshest ingredients, taking the necessary time and care to properly store and prepare the food, and using simple recipes that allow the natural flavor and quality of the seafood to shine through.

One noteworthy caveat regarding seafood preparation involves whether or not to eat it raw. Oysters on the half shell, sushi, and ceviche are three delightful ways to enjoy fish and shellfish, but the US Food and Drug Administration advises that seafood should be cooked to minimize risk of foodborne illness. If you do choose to eat fish or shellfish that is raw or undercooked, be sure that it has first been properly frozen. Although freezing won't kill all germs, it will kill parasites.

CRAB

Anyone who has visited the seafood counter knows that crabmeat doesn't come cheap. For one thing, crab fishing is dangerous and labor intensive. Crab fisheries are strictly controlled, so fresh crab is a limited resource. And of course, a lot of work goes into procuring, storing, preparing, cooking, and cleaning the crab before you're ready to dip the meat into a dish of salted and clarified butter at your own table. Dungeness crabs are often sold whole and live, or whole and cooked. For snow and king crabs, the legs are sold precooked and frozen.

The first decision to make when planning a crab meal, then, is whether to buy a whole, live Dungeness crab, a whole cooked one, or Alaskan king or snow crab legs that have been cooked, cleaned, and frozen.

Whole, live Dungeness crab: If you decide to purchase a live crab, be sure to select a lively one that was harvested in the last two or three days. Avoid any that appear lethargic in the tank or that *don't* mind you reaching in and touching them! Also, be sure they have all eight legs and both pincer claws.

You'll want to cook the crab the same day; experts advise against eating dead crabs that haven't been cooked, even if they died while under your watch, because bacteria multiply fast once the animal dies. To keep it alive, store it in the refrigerator, a cooler filled with ice, or a bucket of cold, clean seawater. Most experts also advise not letting it come in contact with fresh water, and some recommend lining the ice chest with newspaper to prevent the crab from coming in contact with ice made from fresh water.

Some chefs recommend cooking the crab whole and cleaning it afterward. It can be added live to a large pot of boiling water that's been seasoned with your favorite blend of spices—such as bay leaf, celery salt, dry mustard, and paprika—and simmered until cooked through, about ten to fifteen minutes. Or it can be steamed using less water and a steamer basket. Steaming helps preserve the flavor and texture.

Cooks may choose to kill the crab quickly before cooking. To do so, set the crab in the freezer for thirty minutes to numb it. Then carefully pick up the crab by its back two legs (taking care to keep its pincer claws as far away from you as possible) and look at its underside. The crab has two nerve centers, one in the middle of its abdomen and one nearer to its mouth. The goal is to crush the lower nerve center—quickly and with intention—using a sharp object or edge. When the juices drain out and the legs go limp, you'll know you've accomplished your goal. Once you've killed the crab, you can cook it whole or clean it before cooking, adding only the edible portions to the pot.

Alaskan king and snow crab legs: The Alaskan king and snow crabs are often sold as crab legs, rather than whole, with the legs having already been cleaned, pre-cooked, and frozen.

If you find them fresh, be sure they smell pleasant and the meat is white. Avoid any legs that show tinges of blue or gray in the meat, which could mean they were previously frozen and not stored properly. If you're buying frozen crab legs, watch out for crystals as evidence of freezer burn, and keep the legs frozen until ready to use. They can be thawed overnight in the refrigerator or quickly, in just fifteen minutes, if placed under cold running water.

Although crab leg meat has already been cooked, you'll want to reheat and season it to prepare your meal. Legs can be steamed, which better preserves flavor and texture, or boiled like whole crabs, although they will take less time than a whole, live crab. They can also be basted with olive oil or melted butter and baked, broiled, or grilled. The Crab Pot Restaurant steams its Alaskan crab legs for the best flavor results.

Alaskan king, snow, and Dungeness crabmeat is often described as mild, sweet, and buttery, often compared to Maine lobster. (Some connoisseurs also sense a salty undertone in snow crabmeat.) All of these crabs are so delicious that they can be served and eaten simply alongside wedges of fresh lemon, drawn butter, or aioli. If serving plain, you may wish to pick the meat in advance, or you can hand a wooden mallet, some pointed claw tips, and crab crackers—and bibs—to your guests and let them work together to dig the meat out from the shells. Keep in mind that Alaskan king crab leg shells are sometimes hard to crack, so you'll want to be sure you have all the right tools available. Also, whether you do the picking or invite your guests to partake, always be sure that you, or your guests, finger through the meat to be sure no pieces of shell remain.

Of course, crabmeat is versatile and works well in numerous dishes including fresh green salads, spicy crab cocktails or dips, breaded crab cakes, rich cioppinos and other stews, or creamy pasta dishes (including mac & cheese). And, if you've remembered to save your shells and the other parts of your crab to make stock, you can wow your guests with delicious crab bisque.

OTHER SHELLFISH

Shrimp

Spot prawns: Also called spot shrimp, these can be purchased live from a tank or frozen. As with crabs and other shellfish, it's best to purchase live spot prawns within a day or two of harvest, selecting the wriggly ones. And only buy them live if you'll be able to keep them that way until you're ready to cook them (within a few hours) *and* if you'll be able to take on the task of either dropping them into the pot of boiling water, live, or twisting their heads off while they're still wriggling, immediately before cooking. Which step you take depends on your recipe and whether it calls for cooking and serving them with their heads on. If you or your guests are squeamish, you may want to buy your spot prawns frozen, with their heads already removed.

Whether dead or alive, spot prawns and other whole shrimp should be washed before using. Whether or not to peel and devein them depends on your preference and cooking method. The shell protects the flavor and moisture content of the shrimp, but the vein (the black line that runs along the back of the shrimp) serves no culinary benefit. It is, technically speaking, the creature's digestive tract and contains its waste. While it *can* be eaten, the flavor is not appealing, and it can render a gritty texture. Most cooks devein larger prawns but ignore the vein in smaller shrimp.

If you decide to devein, note that it's easier to do before cooking and after peeling. But it can be time consuming depending on how many shrimp you need to clean, so plan accordingly! Simply run the tip of a small, sharp knife down the shrimp's back to loosen the vein and then pull it out. If you prefer to leave the shells on, you can still devein the shrimp by carefully slicing the shrimp shell down the middle of the back and pulling out the vein.

Spot prawns can be boiled, steamed, grilled, baked, sautéed, deep-fried, or even cured. When grilling, start by giving them a quick dip in a savory marinade (for no more than an hour) and then placing them in a wire basket, or stringing them on skewers, to keep them from rolling down between the grill's grates. If deep-frying, it's best to remove the veins and shells first so your guests can dive right in and eat them the moment they are served. Cooking prawns only takes a few minutes, and they are easy to overcook. When they begin to curl and turn pink, and their shells appear pearly opaque, they are done! Never leave them in their cooking liquid after removing them from the heat, as they will continue to cook.

Pink shrimp: These shrimp are normally sold pre-cooked with their heads and shells already removed. They simply need to be rinsed and drained, and then they're ready to do their jobs in your salads and pastas—or in a classic, tangy shrimp cocktail.

Clams, Oysters, and Mussels

When selecting shellfish, choose those harvested within the last day or two, and look for the ones whose shells are whole and closed. Your merchant should be able to tell you exactly when and where they were harvested because all shellfish must be tagged with this information.

Wait to buy your shellfish until shortly before you plan to eat them. Like live shrimp and crabs, live mollusks need to be kept alive until ready to cook or eat. To keep yours alive, store them in the refrigerator or in an ice-packed cooler under a damp (but not wet) towel. Do not put them in fresh water or let them directly touch your ice, as fresh water can kill them. If they came covered in plastic, be sure the plastic is perforated so the animals don't suffocate.

Keep in mind that an open shell *suggests* the animal might be dead, but it's not a guaranteed fact. You can verify this by gently touching the creature. If you do and the shell closes, you're good to go. If not, discard it.

While mussels should be eaten within a day of purchase, clams can last up to two weeks if properly stored. If you are planning to eat your oysters raw, buy them on the same day you plan to eat them. If you're planning to shuck your oysters, note that the ones with smoother shells have been tumbled and will be easier to shuck. But it's also fine to buy oysters already shucked and packed in jars if you're going to cook them rather than eat them raw.

To prepare your clams, oysters, or mussels, start by scrubbing them under cold water with a stiff brush to remove mud and sand, paying close attention to the hinge. If you dug them yourself or bought them from a tank that didn't have circulating salt water, you

may also want to purge them of excess sand by soaking in salt water (not fresh water) for at least twenty minutes, rinsing, and then repeating. If you bought farmed mussels, they were likely grown on suspension ropes and should be easier to clean than wild mussels. Then, you will need to debeard your mussels, which means removing the threads they used to hang on to the rocks or each other. To do so, simply hold the mussel firmly with one hand and use tweezers in your other hand to twist and pull out the threads.

If you're planning to slurp your oysters raw, you'll need to shuck them first. Use a towel or thick glove to hold the oyster in one hand with the flatter side up, and then insert a short, sharp knife into the oyster near the hinge. As you work the knife in, twist it until you hear the hinge pop. Once the hinge has popped open, you can slide the knife between the shells, carefully cutting where the oyster is attached to the top shell. Open the shells, remove the top shell, and slide the knife around the oyster resting in the bottom shell to loosen it.

The general rule of thumb for cooking clams, oysters, and mussels is to cook them just until their shells open and to discard any whose shells remain closed. The hardest part about working with them is deciding how to enjoy them! Manila clams are commonly steamed, but they can also be shucked, grilled in a wire basket or foil pouch, and then munched like popcorn or stirred into pasta. Razor clams are glorious breaded and fried, while geoducks are often served sashimi-style or deep-fried.

Oysters can also be grilled on their half shells or sautéed stovetop with butter, lemon, and herbs. A tried-and-true recipe for oysters dating back to the 1800s is the classic "Hangtown fry," in which the shellfish are served alongside bacon and eggs. They can also be steamed or baked in the shell or shucked and fried, sautéed, or added to stews or chowders.

Mussels steam especially well in wine or a seasoned tomato broth—especially over an open firepit if one is available! They are also delicious smoked.

Squid

Squid can be purchased whole, or you can find them already cleaned or frozen. To prepare a whole squid, begin by laying it on a flat surface and stretching it lengthwise. Cut off the ten tentacles, just below the eye, and pull off the mouth. Remove as much skin as you can from the tentacles and, squeezing the body, pull out the head and transparent center quill. Wash the remaining squid sac well, peeling off the outer membrane, and then slice it into pieces as called for by your recipe.

Squid are versatile and can be grilled, seared in a wok, battered and fried, or poached in butter. The tentacles also make an impressive presentation when stuffed and roasted, and the adventuresome cook might want to experiment with using the squid's ink, from the sac, to add color and savory flavor to a pasta sauce.

Salmon

Although fresh fish, when purchased right off the dock, is phenomenal, it's sometimes better to buy salmon that's been flash- or deep-frozen at sea (FAS) because fish can deteriorate rapidly after it's hauled out of the cold water. If you are planning to buy whole fresh salmon, make sure it's displayed on ice and has clear eyes. The gills should be bright and the flesh shiny and firm enough that it bounces back when pressed. When buying a fillet, make sure it's neither dry nor mushy and it doesn't have dark or greenish hues. Avoid any fish that smells too fishy.

When you get your salmon home, rinse it under cold water, pat dry with paper towels, and wrap in plastic wrap and then foil. Store in the coldest part of your refrigerator and use within two days. The same applies if you caught your own fish, and be sure that, until you get it home, you keep it in an ice-packed cooler in the shade.

Previously frozen fish should be selected from the bottom of the freezer case, and you should avoid any packages with visible ice crystals. Frozen salmon, kept airtight in a plastic or foil package, will keep for up to three months. When ready to use, thaw it overnight in the refrigerator or under cold running water right before cooking. Fish can also be thawed in the microwave on a defrost setting, provided you stop the cycle when the fish still has some ice on it but appears slightly pliable.

When it's time to cook, keep in mind that the connective tissue of fish is made of collagen that is not as strong as the collagen found in land meats, and it will gel at a lower temperature. This is what allows fish to cook at lower temperatures and become opaque and flaky.

Chinooks are high in fat and great for grilling, pan-searing, or baking. Sockeyes offer a flavorful and colorful meat that works well for both grilling and slow roasting. The pink salmon has a more moderate fat content, which makes it especially good for smoking. And because chum has a mild flavor profile, it works perfectly in

saucy recipes that don't need to showcase the fish's inherent flavor.

Even if you choose grilling as your cooking technique, which obviously offers a quick cooking time and easy cleanup, it doesn't mean you should rush the preparation. Some chefs recommend curing the fish first to help retain the texture and flavor and also to help make sure the moisture content remains high even after the fish is removed from the grill. One simple method of curing is to sprinkle a generous helping of salt and sugar, using a 2:1 ratio, on both the skin side and the flesh side of the fillet. Then sprinkle with your favorite herbs, lay the fish on a tray covered with paper towels (skin side up), and store in the refrigerator for as little as one hour or as long as two days (depending on how much time has passed since you purchased it). The longer the fish sits, the more it will soak up the flavors. Eventually, the skin will begin to feel tacky and develop a film, which is what holds in the moisture and promotes caramelization of the sugar.

Salmon and other fish can also be brined, especially before smoking, by mixing salt and sugar into water, seasoning the liquid with garlic, onions, and herbs, and pouring it into a glass dish before immersing the fish. Less salt is used in brining than curing, and the trick is to let it sit long enough for the salt to permeate the muscle—at least twenty-four hours.

And of course, many chefs choose to marinate their fish. Some would argue that a beautiful cut of Chinook salmon should never be marinated; its own flavor should be the honored guest at the table. But a fifteen-to-thirty-minute bath in a tasty, herb-infused, and oil-based marinade adds extra character and enhances the moisture content in most types of fish.

Now that the advanced preparation is done, it's time to cook the fish! To grill, try setting it on soaked alderwood planks atop the grill, wrapping it in foil, or placing it in a wire basket. Salmon also does well slow-roasted in the oven, especially when first rubbed with butter or oil and herbs, as well as steamed or pan-seared. Salmon is a beloved ingredient in many cuisines around the world; there is no end to the cooking possibilities.

Salmon is a popular ingredient in modern-day sushi, as well—although the Japanese did not initially eat salmon raw because the salmon endemic to that region had parasites. Since alternative salmon species have become available globally, salmon is now commonly found on sushi menus worldwide. Finally, a classic, popular way to enjoy salmon is in the form of lox, which is traditionally cured salmon belly and which has roots in both Scandinavian and Native American cultures.

Halibut

Halibut is often sold flash frozen as steaks or fillets, but when it's in season, it can be found fresh. (Delicious halibut cheeks, which are small medallion-shaped cuts, may also be available in season.) Look for thicker cuts from the middle of the fish, which are easier to work with and help you avoid overcooking. Also look for moist, white meat with a clear sheen and a clean (or nonexistent) aroma.

Once you bring it home, your halibut will last in the refrigerator for two to three days. It will also last in the freezer for up to six months, but if you plan to keep it there for more than two months, wrap the original package in an extra layer of plastic, foil, or freezer paper or store it in an airtight freezer bag. Given that halibut keeps well in the freezer, you might consider buying a whole fish when it's in season. It can range anywhere from eleven to twenty pounds and will make a beautiful presentation at any big party on your horizon. Ask your fishmonger to cut it into sizes that work for you and vacuum seal it.

Halibut doesn't need a lot of advance preparation other than basting with herbed butter or giving it a quick dip into a marinade. It does well on the grill because of its thick, firm meat, which holds up nicely and caramelizes over high heat, enhancing its sweet taste. Halibut can also be flipped without falling apart! Other traditional ways to cook halibut include pan-searing, sautéing, baking, and poaching. It is best when cooked using recipes that *add* fat, like buttery or creamy sauces, because halibut is lean and dries out easily. Halibut is also often served in tomato-based stews or raw in ceviche after curing in a medley of lime, peppers, and herbs.

Garnishes

TARTAR SAUCE

Makes about 1½ cups

1 cup mayonnaise
¼ cup dill pickle relish
¼ cup sweet pickle relish
1 teaspoon lemon juice
¼ teaspoon dried dill weed
Pinch of dried parsley
¼ cup water

Of course you could just grab a bottle of tartar sauce off the shelves at your favorite grocery store. But this simple recipe will pay you back in fresh flavor. It's a natural accompaniment to any fish dish and delicious with french fries too.

In a medium bowl, measure out the mayonnaise, both relishes, lemon juice, dill weed, and parsley, and stir until blended. Mix in the water a little at a time until the sauce reaches your preferred consistency.

TIP! What's the Crab Pot's saucy standard? Making things fresh. Making them aesthetically pleasing is another. The Crab Pot serves sauces in a triangle of red cabbage. Two tablespoons per serving is a good place to start.

NOTE: The garnish recipes may make more than enough for one mealtime. Be sure to refrigerate any unused portion and enjoy within 4 days of making.

COCKTAIL SAUCE

Cocktail sauce is the zippy side crucial to a long list of crustacean staples including calamari, crab legs, and oysters—fresh or fried. It's come a long way since it was first concocted to accompany cocktail prawns, hence its name.

_____

In a medium bowl, mix together the chili sauce, ketchup, horseradish, lemon juice, Worcestershire, and Tabasco until blended.

Makes 1 generous cup

1 cup chili sauce
¼ cup ketchup
1 tablespoon horseradish
1 tablespoon lemon juice
1 teaspoon Worcestershire sauce
¼ teaspoon Tabasco sauce

MIGNONETTE SAUCE

Our mignonette sauce gets its tang from vinegar and its kick from hot sauce. It pairs well as a garnish for any oyster or clam dish topped with chopped green onions.

_____

In a medium bowl, stir together the shallots, powdered sugar, and hot sauce. Then add both of the vinegars and the lemon juice, and mix well. Finally, add the cilantro. Mix together until all of the ingredients are combined.

Makes 1 generous cup

¼ cup chopped shallots

¼ cup powdered sugar

1 tablespoon Tapatio hot sauce

⅓ cup apple cider vinegar

⅓ cup red wine vinegar

4 teaspoons lemon juice

4 teaspoons chopped fresh cilantro

CLAM NECTAR

Makes 4 cups

1 cup (2 sticks) butter

6 cups finely chopped yellow onion (about 2 large)

3 cups finely chopped celery (about 8 ribs)

½ teaspoon minced garlic

4 cups water

¾ cup clam base

¼ cup chicken base (from a jar)

1½ tablespoons lemon juice

The blend of thick chicken base and the very specific taste from clam base gives this nectar its complex flavor. The Crab Pot uses it to top off clams and mussels, but it is also a key ingredient in concocting the sauce for **Cioppino** (page 117).

_____

In a large pot over high heat, heat the butter. Add the onion, celery, and garlic, and sear until the onions are sweaty but not yet browning, about 3 minutes. Add the water, clam base, chicken base, and lemon juice. Bring it all to a boil.

TOMATO HERB AIOLI

One ingredient in this spicy aioli that you may not have at the ready is Clamato juice. Named using the portmanteau for clam and tomato, Clamato is the lead flavor of this dip used on the Crab Pot's shrimp tacos and fried calamari. Make plenty and try it out as a sandwich spread too.

Makes about 1½ cups

1 cup mayonnaise
¼ cup Clamato juice
2 tablespoons lemon juice
1¼ teaspoons paprika
1 teaspoon dried basil
1 teaspoon granulated garlic
Pinch of sugar
Kosher salt

In a medium bowl, whisk together the mayonnaise, Clamato, lemon juice, paprika, basil, garlic, and sugar until blended. Season to taste with salt.

TIP! Is granulated garlic the same as garlic powder? Yes and no. See **Pantry and Equipment** (page 35) for all the dirt.

CHIPOTLE AIOLI

Makes 1 cup

2 tablespoons canned whole chipotles in their juice
1 tablespoon water
¼ teaspoon lemon juice
1 cup mayonnaise

Special equipment:

Food processor

Chipotles start their life as simple jalapeños; then they are dried and smoked to become more complex, delivering a smoky sweet heat that the Crab Pot chefs mix with mayo and citrus to top **Salmon Tacos** (page 125). It's a welcome garnish to other fish dishes and a spicy alternative to ketchup with fries.

In a food processor, purée the chipotles, water, and lemon juice. Transfer the mixture to a medium bowl, add the mayonnaise, and whisk together until blended.

> **TIP!** If you find yourself with no canned chipotles in your pantry, look instead for smoked paprika or cayenne pepper; either will fill in the flavor of this aioli. The former is milder and the latter is considerably hotter, so start with a small amount and let your palate decide how much is enough.

PICO DE GALLO

Pico de gallo's mix of chopped raw ingredients is also called *salsa fresca*, Spanish for "fresh salsa." In either case, it translates to a healthy accompaniment that packs a lot of flavor with only a few items. The Crab Pot omits peppers in favor of ground black pepper. It fills in the blank but with less heat.

Makes 1 generous cup

4 small tomatoes, diced small
1 onion, diced small
3 tablespoons chopped fresh cilantro
2 tablespoons lemon juice
1 tablespoon salt
½ teaspoon ground black pepper

In a medium bowl, stir together the tomatoes, onion, cilantro, lemon juice, salt, and pepper until combined. Serve fresh or chilled from the fridge.

TIP! Letting the salsa marinate in the refrigerator for even 15 minutes before serving will give the ingredients a chance to mingle, amping up the overall flavor.

THOUSAND ISLAND DRESSING

Makes about 2 cups

1 recipe **Tartar Sauce** (page 150) or 1½ cups alternate tartar sauce

¼ cup **Cocktail Sauce** (page 151) or alternate cocktail sauce

¼ teaspoon minced garlic

Over one hundred years old, with its origins in upstate New York, this now common dressing is done here the West Coast way. Use it as a salad dressing or as a dip on pretty much whatever you like.

———————————————

In a medium bowl, stir together both sauces until combined. Add the garlic, and mix well.

BLUE CHEESE DRESSING

Blue-veined crumbly cheese is the key ingredient in this rich, creamy dressing that enhances leafy salads and chicken dishes. The blue cheeses encompass a large range from around the globe, but the classics are French Roquefort, Italian Gorgonzola, and English Stilton. Chef's choice!

———————————

In a medium bowl, stir together the mayonnaise, buttermilk, sour cream, blue cheese, lemon juice, pepper, Worcestershire, Tabasco, and garlic until blended.

Makes 2 generous cups

1 cup mayonnaise
½ cup buttermilk
½ cup sour cream
⅓ cup blue cheese crumbles
½ teaspoon lemon juice
½ teaspoon ground black pepper
¼ teaspoon Worcestershire sauce
¼ teaspoon Tabasco sauce
Pinch of granulated garlic

RANCH DRESSING

Makes 2½ cups

1¼ cups buttermilk

1¼ cups mayonnaise

1 (1-ounce) package of Hidden Valley Original Ranch dressing mix or similar dressing mix

The Crab Pot chefs typically like to start from the freshest ingredients, but with this classic American dressing, they start with a pre-blended mix and elevate it with mayo and—wait for it—buttermilk, for a crowd-pleasing dressing or dip. You can use this on top of the **Pacific Northwest Seafood Louie Salad** (page 91).

In a medium bowl, whisk together the buttermilk, mayonnaise, and dressing mix until blended. Chill covered in the refrigerator for 30 minutes to allow dressing to thicken. Stir thoroughly before serving.

HONEY MUSTARD DRESSING

Honey softens the intensity of mustard in the Crab Pot's version of this popular dressing/dip. It's an obvious choice on salads, but the Crab Pot chefs also slather it on burger buns. You can use it on whatever needs a hint of creamy sweet tanginess.

Makes about 2 cups

1¾ cups mayonnaise
2 tablespoons honey
2 tablespoons yellow mustard
1½ teaspoons dried parsley
¼ teaspoon minced garlic
Dash of Tabasco sauce

In a medium bowl, whisk together the mayonnaise, honey, mustard, parsley, garlic, and Tabasco until blended.

GRILLING BUTTER

Makes 1 cup

1 cup (2 sticks) butter, at room
temperature
1 tablespoon Crab Pot Seaspice or
alternate seafood seasoning

The Crab Pot chefs use liquid margarine for their grilling butter. It is easily found at the grocery store in the same section as butter cubes. But you can substitute any butter or margarine you like for this simple butter dip, which is delicious alongside cooked crab or peel-and-eat shrimp.

In a medium bowl, using a mixer, blend butter and Seaspice until well blended. Keep at room temperature until ready to serve, then heat to melt before serving.

BEER BATTER

It's best to use beer, instead of milk or water, in breading batter. The alcohol evaporates faster, which results in a shortened cooking time and a reduced risk of overcooking whatever food the batter is breading. Mix it up to make **Breaded Calamari** (page 78) and **Coconut Prawns** (page 82).

In a medium bowl, combine the flour, Seaspice, and salt. Add the beer and whisk until combined. It will be a little sticky, which helps when using it to bread fish.

Makes about 2 cups

1⅔ cups flour
2 teaspoons Crab Pot Seaspice or alternate seafood seasoning
1 teaspoon salt
1 (12-ounce) bottle of beer, any type

Desserts

STRAWBERRY–RHUBARB CAKE

Makes 2 loaf cakes

For the topping:

1¾ cups sliced rhubarb, fresh or frozen

1½ cups sliced strawberries, fresh or frozen

½ cup sugar

1 teaspoon cinnamon

1 teaspoon red food coloring (optional)

For the cake:

1 (15-ounce) yellow cake mix*

Cooking spray

Vanilla ice cream (optional)

Special equipment:

2 (9 × 5-inch) loaf pans

In the early days of the Crab Pot, the founder, Hal, tasted a strawberry-rhubarb cake that changed his palate. He knew it was meant for his own restaurant's menu as a fruity culmination after a meal of *fruits de mer*. This recipe is an easy version of the cake of Hal's dreams that comes together quickly thanks to a cake mix.

———————

Preheat the oven to 325° F.

For the topping, in a large saucepan over medium-high heat, add the rhubarb, strawberries, sugar, cinnamon, and food coloring. Stirring constantly, cook until the fruit looks like a soupy sauce, about 15 minutes.

For the cake, follow the manufacturer's directions for mixing the batter. Line each loaf pan with parchment paper, and spray cooking spray onto it, bottom only. Pour in the fruit mix first, distributing evenly between the two pans. Next, pour in the batter to about two-thirds full each while distributing evenly between the two pans. Bake until a toothpick inserted in the center of the cake comes out clean or with just a few crumbs, about 45 minutes. Remove from the oven and let cool for a few minutes before turning over onto a serving platter or wooden board. Carefully remove the parchment paper.

Serve warm or cooled with dishes of ice cream.

*Be sure to check what other ingredients your chosen cake mix may need: butter, oil, eggs, milk . . .

TIP! It's doubtful this cake will stick around too long, but if you find yourself with leftovers, it's just as good the next day at the breakfast table. Or freeze the second loaf for a nice surprise later.

THE CRAB POT BREAD PUDDING

Bread pudding is no longer a humble dessert concocted to repurpose stale bread. Here, sourdough and heavy cream come together with apple and a long list of decadent toppings to defy this dessert's rustic appearance. With red food coloring that matches the restaurant's logo, the Crab Pot brands this pudding as their own.

_____

Preheat the oven to 300° F. Prepare a 9 x 13-inch baking dish by spraying it with nonstick cooking spray.

In a large bowl, whisk the heavy cream, half-and-half, eggs, sugar, cinnamon, and vanilla until fully blended. Add the food coloring, if desired. Set aside.

Place half of the bread cubes in one even layer on the bottom of the prepared baking dish. Add the apples, spreading evenly on top of the bread layer. Then add the remaining bread cubes on top as the final layer. Pour the cream mixture on top evenly. Press down lightly so the bread soaks up all the liquid completely, about 3 minutes.

Cover with foil, and bake for 50 minutes. Remove from the oven and allow to cool slightly.

Serve warm or cold, topped with caramel sauce, chocolate sauce, and whipped cream. And, if there is room in the bowl, a scoop of vanilla ice cream.

Makes 9 servings

Cooking spray
2 cups heavy cream
2 cups half-and-half
6 eggs
1 cup sugar
1½ tablespoons cinnamon
1½ tablespoons vanilla
2 teaspoons red food coloring (optional)
3 torpedo bread rolls or equivalent, cubed into 1-inch pieces
3 large Granny Smith apples, finely chopped
Caramel sauce (optional)
Chocolate sauce (optional)
Whipped cream (optional)
Vanilla ice cream (optional)

MUD PIE

This three-ingredient dessert has one age-old rule: you can't tip it over to eat the cookie crust until you've eaten at least half of its creamy dome. Historically, mud pie started out as a chocolatey treat, but feel free to get creative with other ice cream flavors to suit yourself and those you are serving. Most any flavor will delight.

———————————

In a food processor, grind the cookies into fine crumbs. Add the butter and mix until a paste is formed.

In a 9-inch pie pan, layer the bottom only (not the sides) with the crumb-butter mixture to form the base of the pie. Chill the crust in the freezer until it is hard, about an hour.

Meanwhile, let the ice cream stand until it is soft but not runny. Cut large chunks of the ice cream and place on top of the pie crust, pressing down firmly until the ice cream rests evenly onto the crust. Once a large mounded "pie filling" is formed, smooth the top surface with a knife. Cover the entire pie with plastic wrap, and return it to the freezer until the ice cream firms up, about 2 hours.

Slice the pie into eight portions, and serve! If the three ingredients seem lonely, add whipped cream and chocolate sauce to fill out the plate.

Makes a 9-inch pie, cut into 8 delicious triangles

⅔ cup Hydrox cookies (about 8), made into crumbs
2 tablespoons butter, melted
Half or more of 1 (1½-quart) mocha almond ice cream container
Whipped cream (optional)
Chocolate sauce (optional)

Special equipment:

Food processor

TIP! If you don't own a food processor, you can get the same result by placing the cookies in a plastic bag and using a rolling pin to crush them.

Environmental Sustainability Notes

Sustainability has become a critical consideration in the fishing industry. When the Coast Salish and other Indigenous populations were the only people living in the Pacific Northwest, they lived in harmony with salmon, crabs, and other sea life. Marine populations ebbed and flowed with nature's cycles, but long-term prospects for an adequate supply were not a concern.

Once Europeans and other immigrants flocked to the region, circumstances changed. When the salmon canning industry exploded in the late 1800s and early 1900s, the supply of salmon brought in for processing was often greater than what the canneries could handle, leading to tremendous seafood waste. The overzealous fishermen also inadvertently drove the salmon farther out into the ocean, taking them farther from their spawning sites. At the same time, logging and mining operations expanded in the Pacific Northwest, adversely affecting salmon habitat along rivers and streams, and when dams started going up in the 1930s, salmon were prevented from returning to their spawning grounds at all. It was a perfect storm, and the salmon population dropped precipitously. At roughly the same time, Alaska began to identify symptoms of overfishing in its own waters. By the mid-twentieth century, many fish species were suffering from overfishing, and several fisheries were on the verge of collapse.

In 1976, the Magnuson-Stevens Fishery Conservation and Management Act was passed and became the primary law governing marine fisheries in US waters. The goal was to prevent overfishing, rebuild overfished stocks, ensure a safe and sustainable seafood supply, and protect the habitats that fish need to spawn, grow, and thrive. It set standards about fishing methods and harvest limits, and it also extended the US jurisdiction out to two hundred

nautical miles—whereas previously the boundary had been set at just twelve miles—to prevent foreign fleets from coming close to American shores to catch fish without any oversight or regulation.

A subsequent act, in 1996, set forth additional science-based mandates, including standards surrounding fishing vessel safety and bycatch. An update in 2002 focused on how to identify habitats of concern, and another one in 2007 created catch limits and addressed illegal, unregulated, and unreported fishing practices. In 2018, an amendment to the act revolved primarily around recreational fishing guidelines.

This attention to marine sustainability is promising, given that seafood is an environmentally efficient source of protein, and protecting this food source is imperative for us and for generations to come. Improvements, such as the installation of fish ladders in dams and sustainable hatcheries, have helped protect the region's many precious species. According to the National Oceanic and Atmospheric Administration, more than 90 percent of the fishing stocks under their watch are no longer facing overfishing.

However, sea life ranging from mollusks to whales have continued to become increasingly imperiled in recent years due to unusual weather conditions, toxic algae blooms, marine heat waves, and other factors attributed to climate change. As a result, scientists have been reporting unprecedented declines in salmon, cod, and crab populations, and agencies have been closely monitoring, and sometimes closing, fisheries.

As consumers—and stewards of the land and water—one of the best things we can do is make sure we are buying and eating fish that have been sustainably raised and/or caught. This means making sure they have been sourced from US fisheries, which are closely regulated. It means researching to be sure best practices were used to fish with targeted intentions rather than with widespread nets. Trolling, small-scale purse seining, hook-and-line fishing, and using crab pots are generally considered sustainable fishing methods.

The Crab Pot Restaurant keeps sustainability issues on its radar. In addition to securing locally caught Dungeness from their crab-fishing boat, they source much of their salmon from Alaska (helping to protect Puget Sound's fish, which are the primary food source for the local resident orcas). Shellfish come from farms that pay attention to sustainability.

The Monterey Bay Aquarium Seafood Watch (seafoodwatch. org) is an excellent resource for learning more about sustainability

and for finding recommendations about which species are best to eat. They assign classifications of Best Choice, Certified, Good Alternative, and Avoid based on various factors including the condition of the fishery's population, the impact that harvesting a particular fish has on other species and its habitat, and how well the fisheries are being managed.

We can also do our part to take care of the marine environment when we visit it. The ocean and its surrounding landscape may seem invincible, but it is in fact a fragile and interconnected ecosystem. Beaches and intertidal zones are especially vulnerable, and a single footstep by an intruder, in the wrong spot, can cause inadvertent disruption or irreversible harm to the habitat. Our job is to ensure that sea life remains abundant, and the entire landscape remains healthy, so that future generations can know the joy of fishing, beachcombing, or just marveling at the sunset over open water.

Standard Measurement Conversions

All conversions are approximate.

Volume

US	METRIC
1 teaspoon	5 milliliters
1 tablespoon	15 milliliters
2 tablespoons	30 milliliters
¼ cup	59 milliliters
½ cup	118 milliliters
¾ cup	177 milliliters
1 cup	237 milliliters
1¼ cups	296 milliliters
1½ cups	355 milliliters
2 cups (1 pint)	473 milliliters
3 cups	710 milliliters

Weight

OUNCES	GRAMS
8 (½ pound)	227
10	284
12	340
14	397
16 (1 pound)	454

Oven Temperatures

FAHRENHEIT	CELSIUS
275	135
300	150
325	165
350	180

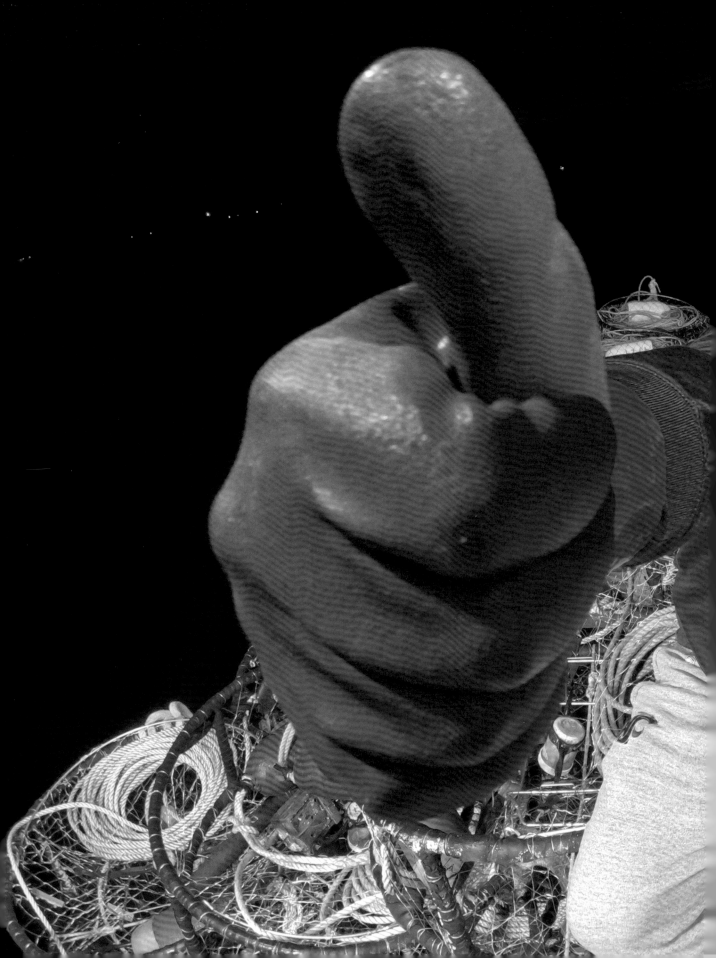

INDEX

About the Griffith Family

The Griffith family is at the forefront of Seattle's waterfront development, led by the visionary Seattle businessman and waterfront developer Hal Griffith. Hal's fascination with a Ferris wheel on Elliott Bay spans nearly three decades, and he, along with his family, owns and operates Pier 57, the home of the iconic Seattle Great Wheel. This bustling pier, known as Miners Landing, also features souvenir gift shops, tourist attractions, and restaurants such as the Crab Pot, offering a delightful experience for locals and tourists alike.

The Miners Landing we know today began in the 1960s, when Hal rented space at Pier 57 for his import business. As an entrepreneur, Hal quickly expanded his ventures, eventually transforming Pirate's Plunder, his import shop, into the largest import store in the Northwest.

Griffith's strong attachment to the historic significance of the waterfront's docks and pier sheds led him to resist the demolition of these structures. Together with other waterfront business owners, the Griffith family played a pivotal role in forming the Seattle Central Waterfront Association to fight for preserving the historic piers, and today, Pier 57 is a designated city landmark. Although their efforts did not prevent the purchase of Pier 57 by the city, their perseverance eventually influenced the city's decision to retain and redevelop most of the piers, including Pier 57. Over the years, the Griffith family has embarked on numerous renovations and expansions, transforming Pier 57 into Miners Landing, a gold rush–themed complex offering restaurants, shops, and attractions.

In June 2012, the Seattle Great Wheel opened at the end of Pier 57, capturing the city's imagination and becoming a prominent Seattle icon.

Kyle Griffith lives in Seattle, Washington, and works alongside his family to run Pier 57, home of the Seattle Great Wheel and Wings over Washington attractions. Kyle is a graduate of the University of Washington, where he developed his passion for the history of the Pacific Northwest. When he's not dreaming up new ways to share his love of Seattle and its past, he's spending time with his wife and two children.

Troy Griffith, the youngest son of Hal, is involved with the operations of the restaurants and buying of seafood and produce. Troy graduated from Washington State University. He and his wife, Ashlie, have four children.

The Griffith family's dedication to the waterfront's development, their relentless pursuit of innovative ideas, and their commitment to Seattle's heritage have left an indelible mark on the city's landscape. Their story is one of vision, perseverance, and love for Seattle's waterfront, which will shape the city's tourism and entertainment scene for generations to come.

From left to right: Joan, Kyle, Hal, and Troy Griffith.